1 MINUTE Biographies

AND ACTIVITIES

Linda Williams Aber

Troll Associates

Metric Conversion Chart

1 inch = 2.54 cm

1 foot = .305 m

1 yard = .914 m

1 mile = 1.61 km

1 square mile = 2.6 square km

1 fluid ounce = 29.573 ml

1 dry ounce = 28.35 g

1 ton = .91 metric ton

1 gallon = 3.79 l

1 pound = 0.45 kg

1 cup = .24 l

1 pint = .473 l

1 teaspoon = 4.93 ml

1 tablespoon = 14.78 ml

Conversion from Fahrenheit to Celsius: subtract 32 and then multiply the remainder by 5/9.

Interior illustrations by Kathleen Kuchera

This edition published in 2002.

ISBN: 0-8167-3275-2
Printed in the United States of America.
10 9 8 7 6 5 4 3 2

CONTENTS

Introduction	v	Maya Lin	52
Susan B. Anthony	6	Christa McAuliffe	54
Arthur Ashe	8	Grandma Moses	56
Alexander Graham Bell	10	Wolfgang Amadeus Mozart	58
Gwendolyn Brooks	12	Florence Nightingale	60
Evelyn Cisneros	14	Sandra Day O'Connor	62
Bill Clinton	16	Rosa Parks	64
Marie Curie	18	Pocahontas	66
Albert Einstein	20	Marco Polo	68
Queen Elizabeth II	22	Diego Rivera	70
Chris Evert	24	Jackie Robinson	72
Anne Frank	26	Eleanor Roosevelt	74
Benjamin Franklin	28	Babe Ruth	76
Galileo Galilei	30	Dr. Seuss	78
Mohandas Gandhi	32	Mother Teresa	80
Jane Goodall	34	Jim Thorpe	82
Virginia Hamilton	36	Sojourner Truth	84
Jim Henson	38	Harriet Tubman	86
Harry Houdini	40	Mark Twain	88
Thomas Jefferson	42	Yoshiko Uchida	90
Chief Joseph	44	Laura Ingalls Wilder	92
Helen Keller	46	The Wright Brothers	94
John Fitzgerald Kennedy	48	Photography and Picture Credits	96
Martin Luther King, Jr.	50		

TO THE TEACHER

One-Minute Biographies introduces your students to a group of men and women thoughtfully selected for their accomplishments, courage, and individuality. Highlights of the lives of forty-six extraordinary people are presented in a short but thorough format. A wealth of across-the-curriculum teaching activities will challenge your students to debate, write, draw, and even conduct experiments related to the biographical subjects. A variety of reproducible activity sheets will further engage each student in the lives of these heroes.

One-Minute Biographies includes summaries of the lives of well-known figures in the fields of science, sports, literature, government, visual arts, music, and exploration. Among those described are: Christa McAuliffe, Albert Einstein, Gwendolyn Brooks, Babe Ruth, Dr. Seuss, Anne Frank, and Jim Henson.

For your convenience, the entries are listed alphabetically. The length of each biography is just right for any attention span: short enough for you to read aloud to the class or for students to read on their own.

After you read through the profiles and decide which ones you would like to share with your class, you can choose from a wide selection of activities that pertain to the biographical subject. A choice of classroom activities follows some of the profiles. Other sketches are followed by individual reproducible sheets. Both classroom and individual activities are related to the featured subject but not necessarily limited to it. You will find many interesting ways to help students boost their skills in literature, writing, public speaking, science, and art while they are introduced to the pleasures of reading biography.

One-Minute Biographies offers positive role models that will inspire your students. They will learn that heroes are not born but shaped by experiences your students will immediately recognize.

SUSAN B. ANTHONY (1820–1906)

Susan Brownell Anthony grew up in the early 1820s in Battensville, New York. With seven brothers and sisters, her family was large and happy. Anthony's education was a mixture of public and home schooling. Her father was a Quaker and educated his children in the Quaker beliefs. One of those beliefs was that women were equal to men. Although others did not always agree, that was what Anthony believed.

Trained to be a teacher, Anthony taught in local schools near Battensville. In 1839, when she was nineteen years old, her father had financial problems. Anthony decided to help with the money she earned teaching. That's when she discovered the terrible truth that changed her life and the lives of all women in the United States. The truth was that women were paid less than men for doing the same job.

Outraged by such injustices as unequal pay for men and women, she wanted to correct this inequality. She became a reformer—someone interested in political and social movements, which included temperance, anti-slavery, and women's rights. In 1851 Anthony met another reformer named Elizabeth Cady Stanton. Stanton had proposed a resolution demanding women's suffrage, or the right of women to vote.

In 1852 Anthony attended a meeting in Albany, New York, where she planned to speak about her concerns. When she was told that "the Sisters were not invited there to speak but to listen and learn," she left and formed a women's organization instead, the first of many she led. She knew very well that unless women could vote and own property, they could not influence political reform movements. She traveled around the country giving lectures on the importance of including all people, not only white men, in the political law-making process. When the Fifteenth Amendment was passed, giving African-American men the right to vote but still not granting women that same right, Anthony and Stanton separated from other suffragists who accepted the amendment.

Anthony decided to test the law to draw attention to her beliefs. In 1872 she was arrested for voting in the presidential election. Her trial brought nationwide attention to women's rights. Anthony was found guilty and fined $100—a fine she never paid.

Her strength and vision brought her to the forefront of the women's movement, which she led from 1892 to 1900. In March 1906 she died, leaving a message for the future: "Failure is impossible." Her work opened the door for the passage of the Nineteenth Amendment in 1920. Fourteen years after Anthony's death, women were able to vote.

ACTIVITIES

Write for What's Right Have students write letters to the President of the United States to share their opinions on issues they feel strongly about, such as education, health care, or equal rights. Whether or not their views are the same as the President's, they'll receive a reply from the White House. Write to: President of the United States, The White House, Washington, D.C. 20500.

Plan a Debate Make up an issue for the class, such as Who Is Smarter: Boys or Girls? Divide the class in half. Let each person give one reason for supporting or opposing the issue. Invite another teacher, another class, or the principal to decide which group won the debate.

Coin a Coin Show the class a Susan B. Anthony silver dollar. Ask students to choose one person whose face they would most like to see on a coin or paper bill. Have them create a motto for the coin or bill and write one or two sentences explaining why they chose that person and what the motto means.

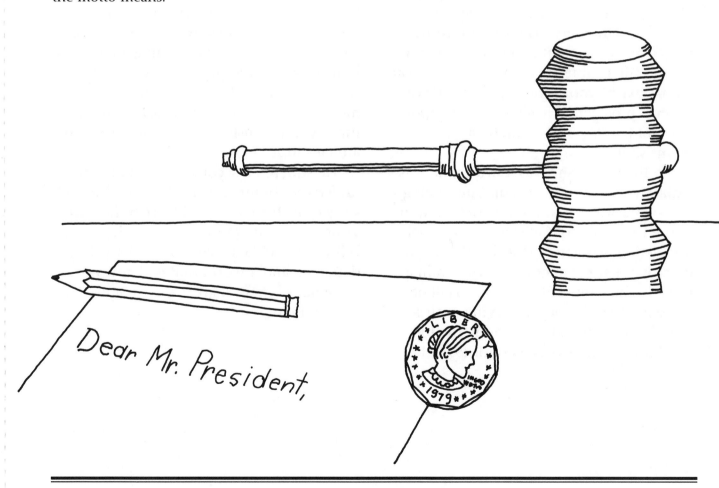

ARTHUR ASHE (1943–1993)

Imagine waking up every day, opening your door, and finding that your front yard is a park and playground. That's what Arthur Ashe, Jr., did as a child growing up in Richmond, Virginia. His father ran the largest park for African Americans in Richmond, and the Ashe family lived right in the park. With tennis courts in his "yard," Ashe began playing tennis when he was seven years old. A part-time tennis instructor recognized the boy's talent and introduced him to Dr. Walter Johnson, an African-American tennis coach who enjoyed helping African-American players. He stressed the importance of tennis-court etiquette as well as tennis skills.

By the time Ashe was fourteen, he was a nationally ranked amateur. After being an honors student in high school, he went to the University of California, Los Angeles, on a tennis scholarship. It was the beginning of a tennis career that earned him a place in the United States Tennis Hall of Fame in 1985. He began playing professionally in 1969 and was among the top five ranked tennis players until 1975, the year he won the Wimbledon Singles Championship and the World Championship Tennis Singles.

Other young men have done very well in tennis, but Ashe was the first African American to reach the top ranks of international tennis. He joined the sport at a time when there were almost no African-American players, and he was not accepted in many of the country clubs where tennis matches were held. Often it took courage as well as talent to play. The first African-American major-league baseball player, Jackie Robinson, encouraged Ashe, but he said his teachers gave him the values and education he needed to succeed.

In 1979 Ashe had a heart attack and was forced to retire from tennis by 1980. Combining his tennis experience and his college education, Ashe became an author, lecturer, and authority on minorities in sports. He spent $250,000 of his own money to produce *A Hard Road to Glory*, a three-volume history of African-American athletes in America.

He suffered a second heart attack and underwent brain surgery as well. During surgery in 1983, Ashe contracted the AIDS virus from a blood transfusion. He died on February 6, 1993, leaving behind a wife, a daughter, and a world that will always remember him as a great athlete and human being.

Name _____ Date _____

Be All That You Can Be!

Arthur Ashe was a tennis player, a writer, and a television commentator at tennis matches. When his tennis career was over, he combined his sports ability and his college education to pursue a whole new career as a sports writer.

Look at the career combinations below. Think of how each pair might be combined to create a third career.

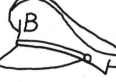

Example: Tennis Player + Writer = Sports Writer

1. **Chef + Teacher** = _____

2. **Inventor + Carpenter** = _____

3. **Doctor + Policewoman** = _____

4. **Firefighter + Airplane Pilot** = _____

5. **Baseball Player + Salesperson** = _____

6. **Nurse + Bus Driver** = _____

7. **Accountant + Computer Expert** = _____

8. **Auto Mechanic + Radio Announcer** = _____

9. **Singer + Childcare Worker** = _____

10. **Lawyer + Social Worker** = _____

ALEXANDER GRAHAM BELL (1847–1922)

Alexander Graham Bell once said that an inventor "can no more help inventing than he can help thinking or breathing." Inventing was that natural to Bell. Best known for his invention of the telephone, Bell held many other patents for inventions. Most inventions had nothing to do with the telephone. Even after a lifetime of inventing, Bell thought of himself mainly as a teacher of the deaf.

Born in Edinburgh, Scotland, on March 3, 1847, Bell was the third generation of his family to study the human voice. His grandfather was an actor and public speaking expert. His father invented a system called "Visible Speech" for teaching speech to deaf people.

After the Bell family moved to Canada in 1870, Bell was sent to Boston by his father to teach the Visible Speech system. He made such a striking impression there that in 1872, he opened his own school in Boston devoted to training teachers of the deaf.

Bell taught during the daytime and worked on electrical experiments at night. He teamed up with an expert in electricity named Thomas A. Watson. Together they worked on creating an instrument that would transmit recognizable words. On March 7, 1876, a patent for the telephone was issued to Bell. Three days later, as Watson and Bell spoke in separate rooms in their Boston workshop, Watson heard Bell's voice saying over the telephone: "Mr. Watson, come here. I want you!"

Bell and Watson's work paved the way for the Bell Telephone Company, which began telephone service in America on July 9, 1877. In the same month Bell married Mabel Hubbard, a young deaf woman.

The success of his telephone company enabled Bell to spend the next forty-five years of his life doing the things he liked best: inventing, working with the deaf, and playing piano. He died near his home in Nova Scotia, Canada, on August 2, 1922.

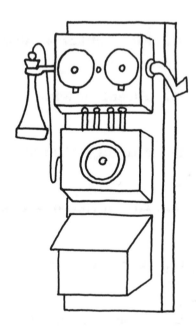

ACTIVITIES

Now Hear This! Put together a sound–test tape of ordinary household noises, and you're guaranteed to hear sounds of student laughter. Tape-record familiar sounds around the house such as: faucet dripping, telephone ringing, cat meowing, dog barking, thunder clapping, door slamming, typewriter typing, clock ticking, tea kettle whistling, dishwasher or lawn mower whirring, people sneezing or snoring. Test students to see who can correctly identify the most sounds.

Bells Are Ringing! Students don't have to ring bells to create their own bell sounds. All they need are four-foot lengths of string and ordinary spoons. Ask each student to tie the string around the spoon handle so that two equal lengths of string are left. Tell them to hold the two loose ends up to their ears like a stethoscope, allowing the spoon to hang freely. When students bend forward so that the spoons hit against the edge of a table, the vibrations will travel along the strings and sound like chimes in their ears.

GWENDOLYN BROOKS (1917–2000)

Gwendolyn Brooks achieved something no other person in the world can ever achieve again. A poet and novelist, she became the first African-American writer to be awarded a Pulitzer Prize. In 1950 her book of poetry *Annie Allen*, which traces the coming-of-age of an African-American woman, won the prize for poetry.

Brooks once said, "Very early in life I became fascinated with the wonders language can achieve. And I began playing with words. That word-play is what I have been known for chiefly."

Her parents encouraged Brooks's interest in writing. Once they noticed that their daughter had talent, they excused her from her household chores and allowed her the time for writing and reading. Her mother suggested that she send samples of her poetry to Weldon Johnson and Langston Hughes, famous poets of the 1920s literary movement known as the Harlem Renaissance. Johnson wrote back encouraging words, but Hughes convinced her of the importance of writing from her own experience. He wanted her to use her African-American background in her writing. She took his advice and set most of her poems and stories in Chicago, where she grew up and has lived most of her life.

Her poetry and her one novel, *Maud Martha*, all focus on ordinary events in everyday life. Her children's book, *Bronzeville Boys and Girls*, is a good example of Brooks writing about her own experience. A book that describes how children feel, it is also about her own childhood feelings.

While her first love was always words themselves, Brooks became more and more intrigued with subject matter. In 1967 she met a group of young African-American writers who had a different goal. They believed that African Americans should write about their own culture and for their own culture. Their attitude influenced Brooks and raised her African-American consciousness, but she has never lost her universal appeal.

In 1985 Brooks became the first African-American woman to be named to the post of poetry consultant to the Library of Congress. Her career has been full of such honors, awards, and prizes. Brooks truly has opened the door for other poets and writers.

Name _____ Date _____

Rhymes For All Times

Gwendolyn Brooks wrote poetry about ordinary events in everyday life. Think about an ordinary day in your life. Write a poem about one simple activity in your day. Examples: waking up early, doing homework, playing with your pet. Don't worry about making your poem rhyme.

EVELYN CISNEROS (1958–   )

With her brown skin, eyes, and hair, Evelyn Cisneros looked different from most of her classmates in Huntington Beach, California. In fact, her whole family looked different. They were Mexican American—the only Mexican Americans living in Huntington Beach. At the age of seven, Cisneros was so painfully shy, she would not raise her hand in class to ask or to answer questions. But it was her shyness that led to her future as an internationally acclaimed prima ballerina.

Her mother enrolled Cisneros in ballet class at the age of seven to help her daughter overcome her shyness. Ballet did that and much more. By the age of eight, Cisneros danced her first ballet solo. Soon she spent all her free time learning ballet, tap, and jazz, which she danced joyously and without a trace of shyness.

From her early teens on, Cisneros was completely devoted to dance, teaching dance every spare minute after school and in summer to pay for her own classes in advanced ballet, tap, and jazz. In her early teens, she received a full scholarship for the summer session at the San Francisco Ballet School. The teachers of this famous company recognized Cisneros's talent and challenged her with more complex dance steps and character roles from well-known ballets.

During her fifteenth summer, Cisneros accepted a scholarship at the New York City Ballet's training school three thousand long miles from home. Disappointed in the level of her classes there, she again spent her next summer with the San Francisco Ballet School, where she became a full-fledged member of the company at the age of eighteen.

In 1979 the San Francisco Ballet's artistic director Michael Smuin created a role specifically for Cisneros in a ballet called *A Song for Dead Warriors*, about the mistreatment of Native Americans. Critics did not agree in their opinions of the ballet, but they all praised Cisneros's performance. Soon after, she traveled with the company to New York and had a fairy-tale experience. Another ballerina in a starring role was hurt, and Cisneros replaced her. Critics raved about her performance, and almost overnight, she became famous.

Since then, she has danced in *Sleeping Beauty, Swan Lake, The Nutcracker Suite*, and many other famous ballets. She also has earned awards from Hispanic Women Making History, the Mexican American Legal Defense Fund, and the National Concilio of America.

Name _____ Date _____

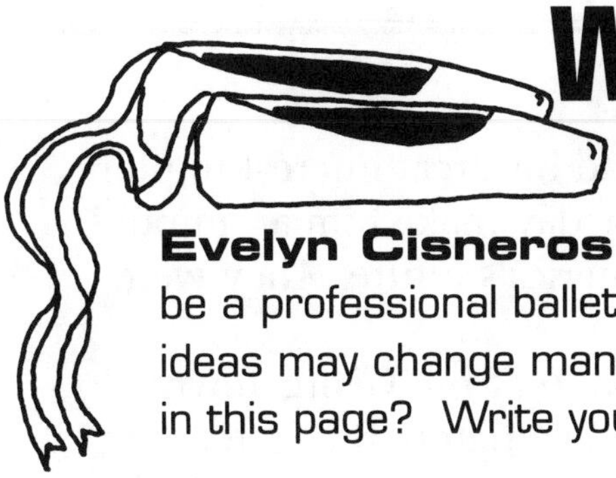

What Will I Be?

Evelyn Cisneros knew by the age of fourteen that someday she would be a professional ballet dancer. What will you be when you grow up? Your ideas may change many times. If you had to decide today, how would you fill in this page? Write your answers in the spaces provided.

When I grow up I would like to be _____

_____

I would choose this because _____

_____

_____

The things I do best are _____

_____

_____

A perfect day for me is one that begins with _____

_____

and ends with _____

_____

The most important thing to consider when thinking about a career is

_____

_____

BILL CLINTON (1946–   )

In the company of names such as Thomas Jefferson, Abraham Lincoln, and George Washington, Bill Clinton may sound ordinary. But Bill Clinton—make that President Bill Clinton—has lived an extraordinary life, ever since he was born on August 19, 1946, in Hope, Arkansas. His father died in a car crash three months before his birth. Clinton's knowledge of his father's death made him determined to accomplish as much as possible. He felt he was living for himself and for his father.

The forty-second President of the United States was named after the father he never knew, William Jefferson Blythe. Shortly after he was born, his widowed mother left him with his grandparents while she went back to school to study nursing. When young Bill Blythe was four years old, his mother married Roger Clinton. Later he changed his name from Blythe to Clinton.

Clinton always did well in school. He learned to read when he was only three years old, and he excelled in academics and music. Saxophone was his main instrument. Those around him believed that his sensitivity to others and his great interest in politics would someday make him an important part of America's future. They were right.

After graduating from Georgetown University in Washington, D.C., attending Oxford University in England, and graduating from Yale Law School, Clinton ran for Congress as a Democrat. He was only twenty-eight years old. He didn't win, but he did gain the title of "wonder boy from Arkansas." In 1975 Clinton married Hillary Rodham, a fellow law student from Yale.

His career soared when he was elected attorney general of Arkansas. In 1978 at the age of thirty-two, he became the youngest governor in America. When he failed to win re-election to a second term, the Clintons were temporarily upset. At the same time, they were greatly cheered by the birth of their daughter Chelsea on February 27, 1980. In 1982 he ran for governor again and won. He became the first Arkansas governor ever to be defeated and re-elected, and the first to serve five terms. His interests were in public education, women's rights, health care, and reduced energy use.

On November 3, l992, the forty-six-year-old governor was elected President of the United States. After a rough campaign the "wonder boy from Arkansas" brought the Democratic party the victory they'd been trying to achieve for twelve years.

Name _____ Date _____

You're The Candidate

Would you like to be President someday? Practice running for office now. Invent a job you want to be elected to at school or at home. Example: Student-In-Charge-Of-Recess or Family Snack Planner. Then design a campaign button and a small poster.

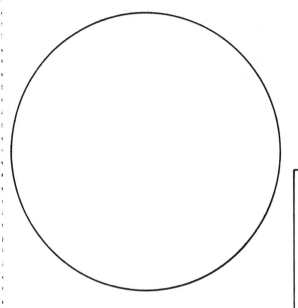

MARIE CURIE (1867–1934)

Marie Curie was a pioneer for women in scientific research. She was the first woman in Europe to earn a doctorate in science. Her discovery that radiation came from inside the atom was her most important find. This information led to a new field called nuclear physics. Curie also discovered radium, which saved or prolonged the lives of millions of cancer patients.

Born on November 7, 1867, in Poland, Curie grew up under Russian rule. Both her parents were teachers, although teaching in Polish was against the law. Because she was a girl, Curie could not go to the university in Poland, so she went to Paris to study. While there, she met Pierre Curie and married him in 1895.

The Curies worked together investigating radiation given off by radioactive substances. They isolated two new chemical elements which they named radium and polonium. In 1903 they shared the Nobel Prize in physics. Pierre died in 1906, but Curie continued the work they began together. She took his place as a professor at the Sorbonne in Paris, and in 1911 she won the Nobel Prize in chemistry. She was the first person ever to receive the award twice.

Throughout her years of working with radioactivity, Curie had an unexplained illness. It was not until after her death on July 4, 1934, that it became clear her illness had been radiation sickness, caused by exposure to radium.

Curie's work paved the way for radiotherapy used in cancer treatments, lasers, and nuclear reactors that generate electrical power. Her discovery also led scientists to the creation of the atom bomb. Curie gave her life to science for the good of humanity.

ACTIVITIES

Are You Curie–ous? Explain to students that as a scientist Marie Curie was curious about the unknown. She did experiments to answer scientific questions. Here are two simple experiments for students to try just for the sake of curiosity.

The Soggy Cereal Test Ask students which breakfast cereal they think gets soggy the soonest. Have students bring in samples of their favorite cereals. Pour equal amounts of different cereals into different bowls. Have several students pour measured amounts of milk into each bowl simultaneously so that the liquid is about a 1/2" below the cereal level. Use a stopwatch to time how long it takes for each sample cereal to absorb the milk completely. Ask a volunteer to write the results on the board after you observe them.

Going in Circles Have a student fill a round dinner plate with water. Ask another student to sprinkle pepper all over the surface of the water. Give a third student a bar of soap with which to touch the center of the water. What happens? The pepper heads away from the soap to the edge of the plate. Explain that the water has a "skin" formed by surface tension. When the soap pushes the tension to the edge of the plate, the pepper follows!

ALBERT EINSTEIN (1879–1955)

Albert Einstein used to get in trouble for thinking. His teachers would look over at him sitting at his desk and see him day-dreaming yet again. Maybe the teachers would not have been so quick to criticize him if they had known that the young daydreamer would grow up to be one of the greatest scientists of all time.

The man whose life changed the world was born in Ulm, Württemberg, Germany on March 14, 1879. Einstein was a quiet, sensitive boy who disliked sports and games. He preferred to observe and study the world around him. When he was five years old, he received a pocket compass from his father. Perhaps this was the beginning of Einstein's curiosity about how the world works. Watching the needle on the compass move because of some out-side force made him wonder about the invisible forces at work in the universe.

When Einstein was twenty-six years old, he introduced his Theory of Relativity. This theory offered scientists new ideas about time, space, mass, motion, and gravi-tation. By using complicated mathematical calculations, Einstein came to the conclu-sion that matter and energy are inter-changeable. His formula, $E=mc^2$, is the equation from which atomic energy was developed. Einstein's theory was one of the elements that went into the making of the atomic bomb.

Einstein spent his life trying to gain a better understanding of physical science. He studied light and energy. Thanks to his studies, such inventions as television and motion pictures became possible. In 1921 Einstein won the Nobel Prize in physics.

Einstein presented his theories and studies to other scientists in Europe and the United States. In 1933 while he was away from Germany, the Nazi government took away all of his property and his citi-zenship. In 1940 he became an American citizen and lived in Princeton, New Jersey, until his death on April 18, 1955.

Name _____ Date _____

Everyone's An Einstein!

Scientists ask a lot of questions. Part of being a good scientist is knowing what questions to ask. Below are some very good answers but no questions! Try to write one question for each answer. There are no wrong questions, only right ones.

1. The solar system. _____

2. At noon. _____

3. A laboratory. _____

4. Top drawer on the left. _____

5. Never in a million years. _____

6. My mother. _____

7. Excellent! _____

8. My own. _____

QUEEN ELIZABETH II (1926–   )

She is a wife, she is a mother, and she is the queen of England. As with all royalty, Queen Elizabeth II did not apply for the job. She was born to it. Her daily life, whether private or public, is guided not by her own personal desires, but by history and traditions. Queen Elizabeth's role as leader of the Commonwealth may surprise those who can only dream of living in a palace. Wearing the crown of the monarch brings with it a lot of work.

The Duke and Duchess of York announced the birth of their daughter, Princess Elizabeth, on April 21, 1926. The tiny princess was third in succession to the throne. Her father became King George VI in 1936 after his brother Edward VIII formally gave up his right to it. This meant that at the age of ten, Elizabeth became heiress to the throne.

Princess Elizabeth accepted the role that was handed to her. She did all that her family expected of her. Her grandmother, Queen Mother Mary, began Elizabeth's training for royal duties. But when she was nineteen, she met Philip Mountbatten, formerly Prince Philip of Greece, and they fell in love. They became engaged, but before marrying Prince Philip, Elizabeth accompanied her parents on a trip to South Africa. She celebrated her twenty-first birthday there with a speech made over the radio to the British people: "I declare before you all that my whole life, whether it be long or short, shall be devoted to your service, and to the service of our great imperial family."

On November 20, 1947, Elizabeth and Philip were married in Westminster Abbey. In 1948 their first son, Charles Philip Arthur George, was born. That same year the King's health began to fail. Elizabeth and her new husband took over many of the royal obligations, including touring the world as his representatives. In 1950 a daughter, Anne Elizabeth Alice Louise, was born. Elizabeth and Philip continued to assume King George's royal duties, but while they were away, King George VI died. Elizabeth was named queen on February 6, 1952, and coronation ceremonies were held on June 2, 1953. Two more children were born: Andrew Albert Christian Edward in 1960; and the last child, Edward Antony Richard Louis, in 1964.

Queen Elizabeth II has reigned for more than forty years. As she promised in her birthday speech, she has devoted her life to serving her loyal subjects.

Name _____ Date _____

My Family Tree

Find out where you fit into your family tree. Ask family members to help you fill in all the
names on this family tree. Add branches if you have a lot of brothers and sisters.

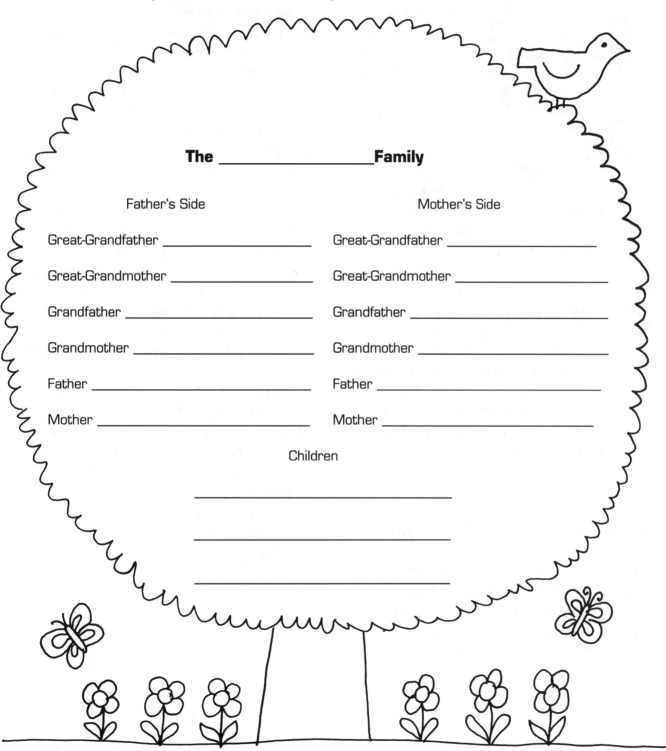

The _____Family

Father's Side   Mother's Side

Great-Grandfather _____   Great-Grandfather _____

Great-Grandmother _____   Great-Grandmother _____

Grandfather _____   Grandfather _____

Grandmother _____   Grandmother _____

Father _____   Father _____

Mother _____   Mother _____

Children

_____

_____

_____

CHRIS EVERT (1954–   )

Tennis, anyone? For Chris Evert's family it's always been tennis every-one! Evert and her four broth-ers and sisters each started playing tennis at five years old. Their father James taught them. All the Everts became good players—but it was Chris who became a world champion.

Growing up in Fort Lauderdale, Florida, meant Evert could practice tennis all year around. Although at times she wished she could go to the beach and relax with her friends, Evert followed a strict practice schedule. She and her brothers and sisters had to practice two hours after school, three hours on weekends, and four hours each day all summer. The practice hours were worthwhile. When she was only eight years old, Evert won her first big ten-nis award.

Between February and September 1971, she amazed everyone by winning twelve tournaments and forty-six matches in a row. The next stop was Forest Hills, New York, for the national championships. Swinging her racket as if it were a baseball bat, she became the youngest player ever to make it to the semifinals. She forced her opponents to run while she stayed at the baseline looking calm and collected. It seemed as if sixteen-year-old Evert might become the Number-One woman tennis player. But in the end, Billie Jean King won the match and kept her title.

From then on Evert put tennis above all other interests. She was determined to be a professional player. In 1972 when she was eighteen, her hard work paid off: she beat Billie Jean King in the Fort Lauderdale Women's International Tournament, adding one more to her collection of 249 trophies. In July of that same year, she went to the most famous tennis tournament of all, Wimbledon. Although Evert lost to Australian tennis star Evonne Goolagong, her career was just beginning. In 1974 she returned to Wimbledon and won. By the end of 1975, the twenty-one-year-old champion had earned prize money totaling $362,227.

On July 30, 1988, Evert married ski champion Andy Mill. Her tennis career lasted until her retirement in 1989. Two years later her son Alexander James was born. A whole new life began for Evert as she moved from the baseline to the sports box where she has gone on to do televi-sion commentary on the game that made her famous.

Name _____ Date _____

What A Fabulous Day It Was!

Winning a game, getting a good grade, celebrating a special event with family and friends—all these things can make a good day great. Write about one of the most wonderful days you've ever had.

One of the best days I've ever had was the day that

_____

_____

_____

_____

_____

_____

_____

_____

_____

_____

_____

ANNE FRANK (1929–1945)

Anne Frank grew up in Germany with a mother and a father who loved her very much. She had an older sister, Margot, who got better grades and was more serious than Anne. She had lots of friends and liked boys, fashion, and ice cream. Anne was like many young girls going to school—that is, until the Nazis forced Anne to be different. When the Nazis came into power in Germany, Anne's whole life changed.

The change started gradually. First, in 1935 Germany took away the political rights of its Jewish citizens. They became foreigners in their own country. The Nazis created laws forbidding Jews to marry non-Jews. All Jewish students were forbidden to go to German schools. By the end of 1938, the Nazis were arresting thousands of Jews and destroying their synagogues and businesses. The Nazis wanted to execute all the Jews in Germany and in the world. Anne and every other Jew in Germany had to start wearing a yellow Star of David on the outside of their clothing so they could be easily recognized as Jews.

In 1933 the Franks moved to the Netherlands to escape the Nazis. But by 1942 life had become too dangerous for Anne and her family. Anne's father Otto decided they would have to go into hiding.

In a building owned by a Dutch woman named Miep Gies, the family lived in a secret attic room for two years without being able to leave. They called it the Annex. The sounds of the outside world were the sounds of war.

During the summer of Anne's thirteenth birthday, her father gave her a present which was to become a gift to the world: a diary. For two years Anne wrote her most private thoughts about life in the storage room. On August 1, 1944, she wrote in her diary for the last time.

On August 4, 1944, Anne and her family were arrested. Someone had betrayed them. The family was separated and sent to different concentration camps. Anne was fifteen years old when she died from typhus in March 1945 in the Bergen-Belsen concentration camp in Germany. The war ended just a few weeks later, too late to save her life.

Name _____ Date _____

Dear Diary

Anne Frank's diary was almost like a close friend. She shared many of her thoughts, feelings, wishes, and dreams with her diary. Share some of your dreams on this diary page.

Dear Diary,

BENJAMIN FRANKLIN (1706–1790)

What did Benjamin Franklin do? Just about everything! He was a printer, publisher, writer, civic leader, scientist, statesman, and one of the smartest Americans ever born. Although his formal schooling ended at the age of ten, he taught himself algebra, geometry, science, logic, writing, grammar, and five foreign languages.

When Franklin was twelve, he became an apprentice to his brother James, who was a printer in Boston, Massachusetts. At seventeen he ran away to Philadelphia, Pennsylvania, and worked for other printers. By 1730 Franklin owned his own print shop. His name became well-known throughout the colonies when he began publishing *The Pennsylvania Gazette* and *Poor Richard's Almanack.*

Franklin was a man who liked to make improvements. Seeing that the Philadelphia postal service was slow and unreliable, he became its postmaster in 1737. Later he became deputy postmaster general for all the colonies. He helped start the first subscription library in the American colonies and improved Philadelphia's services by organizing a fire department, police department, a hospital, and a school that grew into the University of Pennsylvania.

As a scientist and inventor, Franklin invented bifocal lenses, the Franklin stove, and the lightning rod. He proved that lightning is actually electricity. As a public servant, he created a Plan of Union to bring the colonies together under one government. The plan was not completely accepted, but parts of it were later included in the United States Constitution.

In 1775, when the new nation was being organized, Franklin was chosen by the Continental Congress to be Postmaster General. He helped write the Declaration of Independence and was the only man to sign all four of the most important documents written at the time: The Declaration of Independence, the treaty of alliance with France, the Treaty of Paris, and the Constitution.

Franklin died on April 17, 1790, and was buried next to his wife in Philadelphia.

Name _____ Date _____

Mix And Match Maxims

Benjamin Franklin offered many words to the wise in his publication, *Poor Richard's Almanack*. Some of his sayings were original and some rephrased. Many are still quoted today. How many do you know? Draw a line from column 1 matching up the first half of the proverb with the correct second part in column 2.

Column 1

1. Early to bed and early to rise

2. A penny saved

3. Little strokes

4. Lost time

5. The early bird

6. A stitch in time

7. A rolling stone

8. A fool and his money

9. Neither a borrower

10. A word to the wise

Column 2

is never found again.

makes a man healthy, wealthy, and wise.

nor a lender be.

are soon parted.

fell great oaks.

is sufficient.

is a penny earned.

catches the worm.

gathers no moss.

saves nine.

GALILEO GALILEI (1564–1642)

Back in 1581 a young medical student named Galileo Galilei supposedly made a simple observation while sitting in a cathedral in Pisa, Italy—an observation that may have changed the direction of Galileo's life from medicine to physics, as well as the world's understanding of physics itself.

Young Galileo had finished his studies of Latin, Greek, mathematics, religion, music, and painting. He then enrolled as a medical student at the University of Pisa. He was going to be a doctor, but his plans changed the day he looked up at a lamp swinging overhead in a cathedral. He noticed that each swing of the lamp was equal in time no matter how great or small the swing. This law of the pendulum was used to regulate clocks for the next 250 years, until electricity replaced most pendulums. Galileo's discovery led him to a discovery about himself as well. He realized he was more interested in physics than medicine.

Although financial hardship caused him to leave the university before he graduated, Galileo mastered physics and mathematics with the help of a family friend. His inventions were well received, including the telescope to see the stars, the thermoscope to measure heat, and the *sector*, a type of draftsman's compass still used today. But he also was working on the Copernican theory, which said that the earth is not the center of the universe. The pope of the Roman Catholic church tried to stop Galileo from upholding it. As a scientist and physicist, Galileo was always in search of the truth. The church and science disagreed on what the truth was.

In 1632 Galileo published a bestselling book called *A Dialogue On the Two Principal Systems of the World.* The church was offended, and the pope ordered the sixty–eight-year-old Galileo to appear before the Holy Office of the Inquisition. For his beliefs he was confined to his house for the rest of his life and forbidden to speak or write about the Copernican theory. He lost his freedom and his eyesight, but still he continued to write about the laws of force and of motion. His last book was *Dialogues on the Two New Sciences*, which gave Sir Isaac Newton important information that led to his discovery of the laws of gravity.

Galileo died in 1642, but he was not formally pardoned by the church until 1965. In 1979 Pope John Paul II declared that Galileo may have wrongly suffered at the hands of the church.

Name _____ Date _____

A Lighter Look At Gravity

Galileo studied gravity and discovered the Law of Falling Bodies. He proved that no matter what their weight, all bodies or objects are pulled to earth by gravity at the same speed.

Imagine what life would be like if, for just one day, gravity suddenly was gone. In the space below, write your description of "The Day Gravity Disappeared."

_____

_____

_____

_____

_____

_____

_____

_____

_____

_____

_____

_____

_____

MOHANDAS GANDHI (1869–1948)

Most of the pictures of Gandhi show a small, frail-looking man with his head shaved and a wise expression on his face. Yet this one individual helped free India from British rule. A man of great ideas and strong principles, Gandhi used truth and nonviolence to gain the rights he knew all Indians deserved. He was even willing to die for those rights. Instead of using physical violence, he protested nonviolently by fasting—going without food. He would fast for many days until his requests were met. The people of India called him the Mahatma, or Great Soul. He will always be honored as the father of their nation.

Gandhi was born on October 2, 1869, in Porbandar, India. His parents' religious rules were so strict that Gandhi sometimes rebelled. Once he stole a gold coin from his older brother. Afterwards he felt terrible and wrote a letter of confession to his father. Gandhi watched tears fall from his father's eyes as he read the letter. Then his father tore it up as a sign of his love and forgiveness. This simple act taught Gandhi a lesson for life: the power of love and forgiveness has no limits.

When Gandhi was thirteen, he married a girl the same age in a marriage their parents had arranged. But he continued his schooling, and when he was eighteen he studied law in London. In 1893 he went to South Africa to work. While there, he suffered abuse and discrimination because he was Indian. He stayed in South Africa for twenty-one years working for Indian rights. He returned to India in 1915, and within five years became the leader of the Indian nationalist movement.

Gandhi could organize masses of people and lead them in nonviolent acts in order to gain or keep their rights. Although many Indians died at the hands of the British, most Indians did not strike back. Gandhi spent seven years in prison for his attempts to free his country from British rule. In 1947 he achieved his greatest goal: Great Britain granted India its freedom.

"My mission is not simply the brotherhood of Indian humanity," Gandhi wrote. "My mission is not merely freedom for India. But through the freedom of India, I hope to realize and carry on the mission of the Brotherhood of Man."

On January 30, 1948, Gandhi, the Mahatma, was assassinated by an Indian who represented a group that feared his insistence that people of different religious faiths can and should live together in peace. Guided by the search for truth, Gandhi believed that truth could only be realized through love and understanding for his fellow man. Gandhi died, but his example inspired another man famous for nonviolent solutions to problems—Martin Luther King, Jr.

Name _____ Date _____

Gandhi's father once forgave his son by tearing up his confession to a family theft. Gandhi saw his father's action as an example of *ahimsa*, an Indian expression that means "love and nonviolence." Show your understanding of ahimsa by writing down a loving and nonviolent solution to the problems below.

1. Tracy borrowed her sister Jonelle's new skates without asking. Tracy fell and scuffed up both skates. When Jonelle found out, here is what she did:

_____

_____

_____

_____

2. Luke was walking home when the school bully caught up and pushed him for the third time in a week. Luke was embarrassed and angry. But he looked the bully right in the eye and said:

_____

_____

_____

_____

JANE GOODALL (1934–   )

Jane Goodall was only seven years old when a book called *The Story of Doctor Dolittle* influenced her life. The book is a fantasy about an English doctor who talks to animals and travels to Africa to help them. The story made Goodall decide that someday she, too, would leave England and go to Africa.

After Goodall had graduated from secretarial school, a friend invited her to come for a visit in Nairobi, Kenya. Goodall found a secretarial job there and stayed. It wasn't long before she met the famous anthropologist Louis Leakey. He hired her as his secretary and asked her to accompany him and his wife on their search for evidence of early humans in Kenya. Leakey suggested that Goodall begin a scientific study of a group of chimpanzees with funding from the National Geographic Society. Her job was to watch the wild chimpanzees and write down everything she saw them do.

Goodall got up early every morning to look for chimpanzees. Sometimes she would act like one of them so they wouldn't be afraid of her. She learned to swing from branches and walk like a chimpanzee. She picked the same fruits from trees. She even tasted the same insects they ate! It took a long time for the chimps to accept Goodall, but eventually they ate out of her hand. Each chimpanzee became so special to her that she gave them names.

After she married and had a baby, Goodall stayed in what is now the Gombe National Park in Tanzania where she studied the behavior of the chimpanzees. She wrote books such as *My Friends, the Wild Chimpanzees* and established in Arizona the Jane Goodall Institute for Wildlife Research, Education, and Conservation. In the mid-1980s, she started a program called ChimpanZoo in which students study the behavior of chimpanzees in zoos.

Goodall now lives by herself in Tanzania where she has spent more than thirty years. Her work has earned her many wildlife and conservation awards. She is recognized all over the world as one of the foremost animal behaviorists of our time.

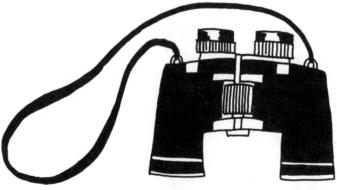

ACTIVITIES

Map Studies On a world map, point out East Africa. See if the students can locate Tanzania. Show them where England is. Using the scale for miles or kilometers, let them estimate how far Goodall traveled from England to Tanzania.

Animal Studies Have each student choose a particular animal to study. Instruct them to find out information about the animal, such as its environment, its living and eating habits, and its life span.

Creative Studies Encourage students to write a journal page about a dream for their own future. What will they do when they grow up? Where will they live? What would be their dream come true?

More about Jane Goodall Suggested further reading.
   The Chimpanzee Family Book, Jane Goodall, Picture Book Studio.
   My Life with the Chimpanzees, Jane Goodall, Pocket Books, Simon and Schuster.

VIRGINIA HAMILTON (1936–   )

Award-winning author Virginia Hamilton makes writing books for children look almost as easy as reading books to children. She is so skilled at making words flow naturally that her readers may miss the fact that each of her thirty books is carefully crafted.

Hamilton always tries to put into words what she learns from life. She not only works at writing, she works at living and observing how others live. Human experience is the source material and subject of all Hamilton's books. Focusing her great imagination on real–life situations, she creates stories rich in characterization. Whether her main characters are boys or girls, young or old, real or imagined, her goal is to bring people together.

She writes often of the African–American experience, but she does not restrict herself. She believes that a writer must have the freedom to write about all subjects, just as the reader has the freedom to read about all subjects.

The wide range of subjects in Hamilton's books shows that she is not afraid to tackle new territory. Her books include romance, mystery, fantasy, history, and mythology. From short stories to anthologies to biographies to novels, Hamilton has raised the standards for children's literature as few other authors. Her books have won many awards, including the coveted Newbery Medal for *M.C. Higgins, the Great* in 1975.

"Writing has to be fun for me," she has said. And if it is fun for her, she hopes that her readers will respond enthusiastically. Judging by the popularity of such young adult books as *Sweet Whispers, Brother Rush; A White Romance; In the Beginning;* and many others, Hamilton's hopes have been realized.

Name _____ Date _____

My Favorite Book Award

A Newbery Award is given each year for the best children's book. Virginia Hamilton won the Newbery Medal for her book *M.C. Higgins, the Great* in 1975. Can you think of a favorite book of yours that deserves a medal? Write about it below.

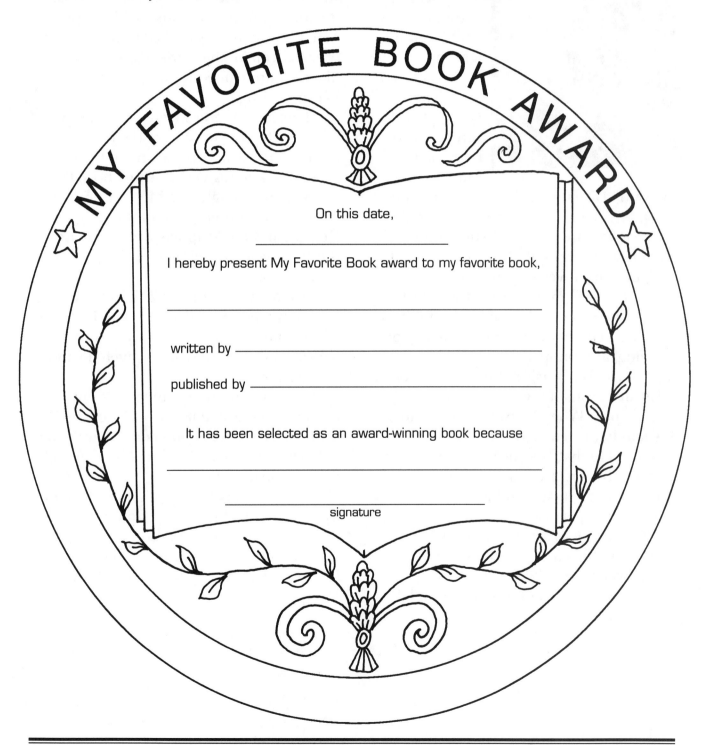

★ MY FAVORITE BOOK AWARD ★

On this date,

_____

I hereby present My Favorite Book award to my favorite book,

_____

written by _____

published by _____

It has been selected as an award-winning book because

_____

_____
signature

JIM HENSON (1936–1990)

Question: What do you get when you cross a puppet and a marionette? Answer: You get a Muppet!

In fact, you get a whole world of creatures created by master Muppeteer, Jim Henson. His famous friends, Kermit the Frog, Miss Piggy, and Fozzie Bear, just to name a few, are perhaps better known than Henson himself. None of the Muppets, however, would be where they are today—TV, movies, stores, and just about everywhere else—if it had not been for Henson's childhood interest in art, performing, and puppet shows.

Jim Henson was born on September 24, 1936, in the small town of Leland, Mississippi. When he was in fifth grade, his family moved to Hyattsville, Maryland. It was there that Henson's fascination with puppets began. He joined his high school's puppet club and gave shows with his own puppets.

When he was seventeen years old, Henson got his first job in television as a puppeteer for a children's show in Washington, D.C. But it wasn't until he went to college at the University of Maryland that his own Muppets made their first appearance on a local Maryland station under the name of *Sam and Friends*. It starred a funny-looking, bald puppet named Sam and his odd collection of friends. One of those friends was a lizard-like creature named Kermit who later became a frog.

Henson's Muppets were created especially for television cameras, which can catch every facial expression. In the early 1960s, the famous variety show host, Ed Sullivan also caught the Muppets' movements and featured them on his show. Henson and the Muppets were regulars on the *Today Show*, the *Ed Sullivan Show*, and the *Tonight Show*.

In 1969 the next big break came for the Muppets when *Sesame Street* invited Henson and his puppet pals to join the show. Seven years later they were given a show of their own.

Henson had three families: his family of Muppets, a creative family of fellow Muppeteers, and his immediate family: his wife Jane and their children, Lisa, Cheryl, Brian, John, and Heather.

Everyone was surprised and saddened by Henson's sudden death from pneumonia on May 16, 1990. His son Brian now carries on the work his father began, and fans everywhere carry on their love for the Muppets.

Name _____ Date _____

Puppet Design Studio

Jim Henson, the master Muppet-maker, always began with a drawing of his idea for a new Muppet. Can you design some puppets for this puppet theater?

HARRY HOUDINI (1874–1926)

If ever there was a person who could make an audience believe in magic, it was Harry Houdini. At every performance, the master magician appeared, disappeared, and escaped from impossible situations while convincing everyone that he was facing possible death. There were no chains, ropes, handcuffs, or locks that could hold him. The only one who could outdo the Great Houdini was Houdini himself. But it was hard work, not magic, that made him the most world-famous escape artist who ever lived.

Houdini was born Ehrich Weiss, the son of a rabbi in Budapest, Hungary. When he was still young, his family moved to Appleton, Wisconsin, where his father led a small group of Jewish people. Rabbi Weiss did not earn much, so young Ehrich and his brothers took odd jobs to bring in extra money. He also began teaching himself magic tricks, many of which involved escaping from ropes. Before long, he was performing magic for money. He changed his name to Houdini after Jean Eugene Robert-Houdin, a great French magician.

Houdini's younger brother was also interested in magic. They created an act called "The Brothers Houdini" and performed in small theaters, at parties—wherever they could. They took the act to Coney Island, where Houdini met and married Beatrice "Bess" Rahner. Tiny enough to fit into the trick trunks and boxes used for escape illusions, she replaced his brother in the act. The couple became known as "Master Monarchs of Modern Mystery."

At first, Bess and Harry Houdini performed in and around New York without much success. So Houdini developed more daring, more amazing feats of magic and publicized his tricks in advance. He added seances to his act, convincing people that he was capable of talking to the spirits of the dead. But it bothered him to fool people into thinking he could give them messages from their lost loved ones. He not only quit doing seances, he started exposing others in that field.

As he perfected his magic and the art of escape, Houdini became a huge success in Europe. By the age of thirty-eight, he was the best-known magician in the United States.

In 1926, in Montreal, Canada, a young college boxer came to Houdini's dressing room. The boxer asked if he could test Houdini's famous strong body with a punch to the stomach. Houdini took the punch. But the next day, he became sick with a high fever and died of a torn appendix. The master magician was gone, leaving behind a library of 5,200 books on magic and a reputation that lives on.

Answer for page 41: The final answer is always three.

Name _____ Date _____

Be A Math Magician

Harry Houdini was a great magician. He worked hard teaching himself the tricks he performed. Here's a trick you can do to amaze your friends, your family, and maybe even yourself! This trick works every time. Try it three times and you'll see.

	1st Try	**2nd Try**	**3rd Try**
1. Pick any number.	___	___	___
2. Add nine to the number.	___	___	___
3. Double the new number.	___	___	___
4. Subtract twelve.	___	___	___
5. Divide the answer by two.	___	___	___
6. Subtract the original number.	___	___	___
7. Write the number that is left.	___	___	___

What do you notice at the end of each math trick?

_____

Answer on page 40

THOMAS JEFFERSON (1743–1826)

When people tour Thomas Jefferson's house today in Virginia, they are amazed to hear that his library of more than 6,400 books became the start of the Library of Congress. They are astonished to see examples in each room of his remarkable inventions, from the swivel chair to the seven-day clock. They are eager to learn more about the third President of the United States, an architect who designed the University of Virginia, the Virginia Capitol, and his home, Monticello. It becomes clear that Thomas Jefferson was an extraordinary President and citizen.

Education was the key to Jefferson's success. Born at Shadwell, the family farm in Albemarle County, Virginia, he did not lead the usual farm boy's life. His family was wealthy and educated. His father served as a member of the House of Burgesses, and his mother came from one of the oldest families in Virginia. Jefferson's education included reading, writing, accounting, Latin, Greek, French, and music. He went to the College of William and Mary at Williamsburg and went on to study law. The time he spent with other cultured men helped him form the ideas on which he based the Bill of Rights.

He married Martha Wayles Skelton in 1772 and settled with her at Monticello, the house he designed and had built at Shadwell. They had one son and five daughters, but only two, Martha and Mary, lived to adulthood. One of the most painful events of Jefferson's life was the death of his wife after only ten years of marriage. He never remarried.

Although his law practice was very successful, Jefferson was more interested in public service. Soon he turned all his attention to the government. In 1769 Jefferson was elected to the House of Burgesses. He next served as governor of Virginia, congressman, minister to France, secretary of state, and Vice-President under John Adams. His strong views about the American colonies' right to be independent led to his writing the Declaration of Independence, which was signed on July 4, 1776.

Jefferson's two terms as the third President were eventful in United States history. The purchase of the Louisiana Territory doubled the size of the country. Chief Justice John Marshall established the Supreme Court's power of judicial review.

In 1809 Jefferson decided not to run for a third term as President. He retired to Monticello, where he experimented with new farming techniques. He also founded the University of Virginia. Thomas Jefferson died on the same day as his old friend John Adams: July 4, 1826, exactly fifty years after the signing of the Declaration of Independence.

ACTIVITIES

Start a Library Thomas Jefferson donated his collection of 6,400 books to begin the Library of Congress. Have each student make a book cover of his or her favorite book. Make a "Library Bulletin Board" using all the students' book covers. Create the ideal library by having each student make up a list of his or her top-ten favorite books. Make up one master list. As students read other books, they can add them to the ideal library list.

Invention Convention Organize a mini-Invention Convention. Have each student invent something that fills a need. Jefferson's dumbwaiter carried dishes to and from the kitchen. His seven-day clock kept time for seven days without winding. Have students make a drawing, a model, and give an oral report explaining why the invention is necessary and how it works.

Declare Independence Discuss the Declaration of Independence and its importance in American history. Why did the colonies want their independence? How would life improve for the colonists? Are there any advantages for a colony in staying dependent on a powerful country?

CHIEF JOSEPH (1840–1904)

In 1840 in Oregon's Wallowa Valley, a son was born to a Nez Percé chief and his wife. The child's tribal name meant *Thunder Rolling in the Mountains*. Growing up as the son of a chief, the youth saw that his father's greatest challenge was to hold onto the tribal lands in northeastern Oregon and keep them out of the hands of the white settlers.

At the age of thirty-one, the young man became Chief Joseph, new leader of the Nez Percé tribe in the Wallowa Valley. A towering figure, he stood 6'2" and weighed 200 pounds.

Since their contact with French trappers in 1750, the Nez Percé tribe had lived in peace with white people. When the explorers Lewis and Clark entered Nez Percé territory in 1805, they were greeted warmly. Chief Joseph's people were proud that they had never killed a white person. But as white settlers streamed into the tribe's land, the newcomers claimed it as their own. By 1871 when Joseph became chief, it was clear that the settlers' demands would not be satisfied until they had all the land at their disposal.

Chief Joseph was a peaceful man, whose greatest wish was to keep what rightfully belonged to his people without going to war. But in 1875, President Grant granted white homesteaders the right to settle in the Wallowa Valley. The settlers built roads and bridges, and soon even the government's army could not keep them from stealing horses, cattle, and land from the Nez Percé.

Trouble really started when two ranchers shot and killed a young Native American boy accused of stealing their horses. General Oliver Otis Howard ordered the tribes to move to the reservation within thirty days. A small band of young Native Americans decided to get revenge by raiding white settlements. For the first time, Nez Percé killed whites. The Nez Percé War had begun, and it lasted through the summer and fall of 1877.

Although the Native Americans were outnumbered, Chief Joseph was a military genius when it came to fighting. He fought off the government troops and led his people more than one thousand miles through Washington, Idaho, and Montana, where he was finally forced to surrender forty miles from the Canadian border. As he handed over his rifle, he said, "From where the sun now stands, I will fight no more forever."

Chief Joseph spent the last part of his life on the Colville Reservation in Washington state, living in a tipi instead of the government-provided house. As the great leader sat by his fire on September 21, 1904, he collapsed and died. The doctor gave the cause of death as "a broken heart."

Name _____ Date _____

The Earth Is A Treasure

The earth belongs to everyone, and we are all responsible for keeping it clean. Make a poster to remind people that the earth is our most precious treasure.

HELEN KELLER (1880–1968)

Imagine a world without sound and without sight. No music, no colors, no voices, no faces. This was Helen Keller's world. Before she was two years old, a serious illness plunged her into silence and blindness. The door to the outside world was suddenly closed to her, but Keller found the strength to open it for herself and for thousands of other physically-challenged people.

Keller was born June 27, 1880, in Tuscumbia, Alabama. After her illness, she spent the next five years adjusting to being deaf and mute. Without the ability to hear and imitate speech, she created her own sounds to express herself. To show pleasure she made a chuckling, giggling sound. To show anger or displeasure she kicked, scratched, and made guttural sounds like choked screams. Her wildness became unbearable to her parents. Her father had heard of Alexander Graham Bell's work with the deaf. He took his daughter to see Bell, and that was the beginning of a long friendship between Keller and Bell. Bell advised the Kellers to contact the Perkins Institute for the Blind in Boston to find a special teacher.

Just before Keller turned seven, her teacher Anne Sullivan arrived from Boston. Sullivan first had to gain the young girl's trust. But how could she do that when Keller could not see her face or hear her voice? Sullivan used the sense of touch to reach her pupil's mind. She introduced herself by allowing Keller to touch her face and feel her mouth as she spoke. She spelled out words on Keller's hand using a finger alphabet. The process was slow, but gradually the child was able to connect words with the objects they described. Within three years she learned the alphabet and could read and write in Braille on a special typewriter made just for her.

When she was ten years old, Keller decided that speaking in sign language was not enough. She wanted to talk, so she took lessons from a teacher of deaf people. Her progress was remarkable. By the time she was sixteen, she could speak well enough to go to a college preparatory school and then to Radcliffe College. She graduated with honors in 1904.

Keller used her own experience to help improve living conditions for other physically-challenged people all over the world. During World War II she visited soldiers blinded in battle. She lectured and raised money for the Helen Keller Endowment Fund which benefited deaf and blind people. She wrote many articles and books. Perhaps the most famous work about Keller is William Gibson's Pulitzer Prize play *The Miracle Worker* (1959; film, 1962). It tells how the lifelong friendship between Sullivan and Keller first began. Helen Keller died on June 1, 1968, after a long and successful life.

Name _____ Date _____

Seeing With Your Fingertips

Helen Keller was blind, yet she was able to read, write, and finish college. Louis Braille's invention of an alphabet for blind people helped Keller. Using their sense of touch, the blind feel tiny bumps to identify each Braille letter. Can you read the Braille alphabet? Practice learning each letter. Then try to write your name or a word in Braille below.

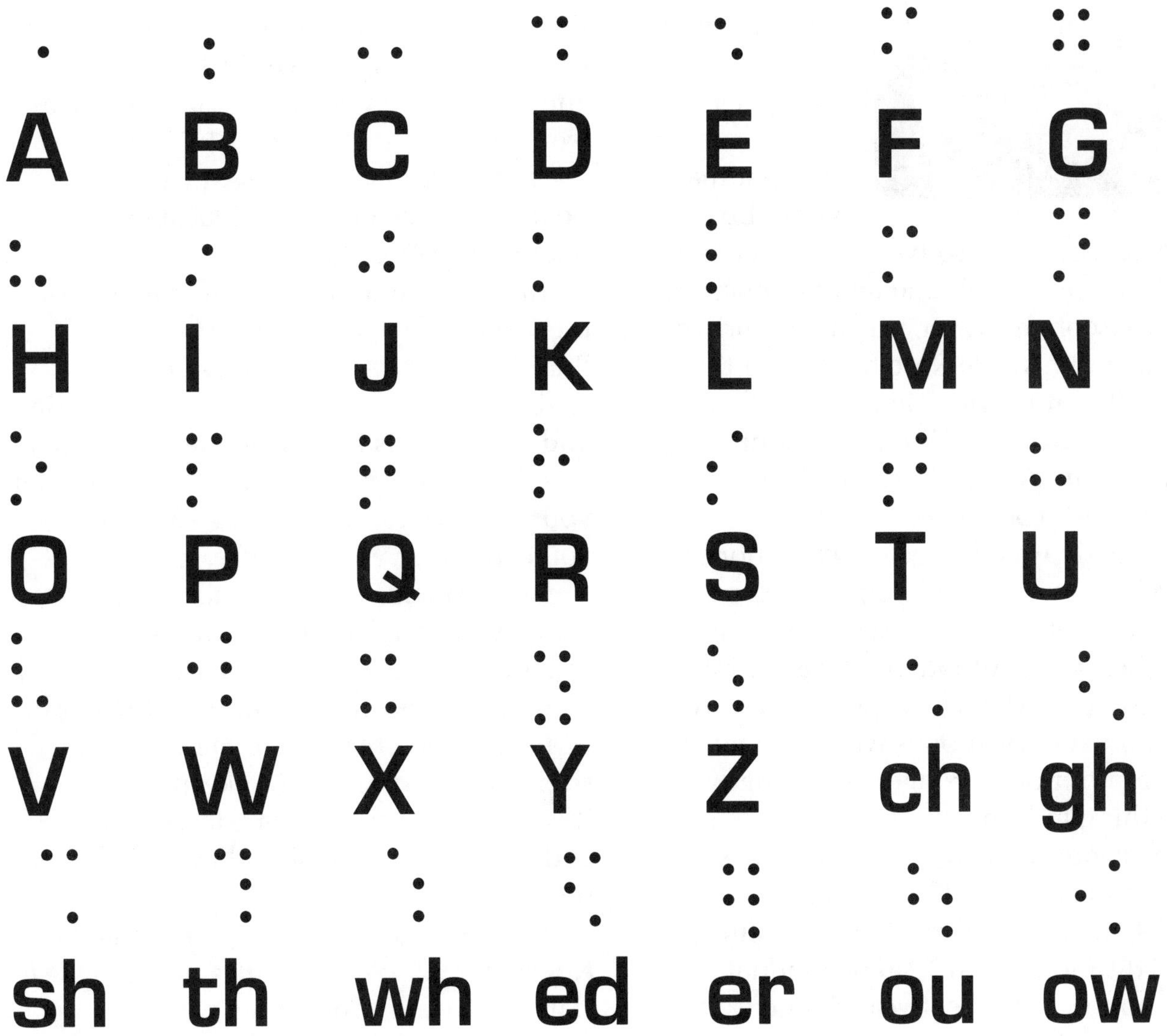

A B C D E F G

H I J K L M N

O P Q R S T U

V W X Y Z ch gh

sh th wh ed er ou ow

_____

_____

_____

JOHN FITZGERALD KENNEDY (1917–1963)

When John F. Kennedy was sworn in as the thirty-fifth President of the United States, many people were surprised. At forty-three years old, he was the youngest man ever to be elected President. He also was the first Roman Catholic ever to hold the highest office. His father Joseph, however, was not surprised at all. He and his wife Rose had raised their nine children to win. He was sure that one of his sons would be President. John Kennedy, nicknamed "Jack," made his father's wish come true.

Kennedy was the second child born to the rich, powerful, and politically connected Kennedys. As a boy, Kennedy was thin and often sick. Although he was so frail, Kennedy played hard at sports. He was determined to beat boys who were much bigger and much stronger. Winning was everything to him.

In school Kennedy was not always a very good student. It wasn't until his third year at Harvard University that he finally studied seriously. In 1940 he graduated with honors. The next year Kennedy joined the Navy. Three months later Japanese bombers attacked U.S. ships and planes at Pearl Harbor, Hawaii, bringing the United States into the war. Kennedy was the commander of a Navy boat called PT-109. When his boat was hit by a Japanese destroyer, Kennedy swam to safety while carrying an injured crew member. This earned him a medal of bravery.

With the help of his whole family, Kennedy ran for a seat in the United States House of Representatives in 1946. He won and was a congressman for six years. He won a seat in the Senate in 1952 and was re-elected in 1956. On his way up the political ladder, he married Jacqueline Bouvier in 1953.

In 1960 Kennedy was nominated to be the Democratic party's candidate for President of the United States. He ran against then Vice-President Richard Nixon and won. In his famous inaugural speech he told the American people, "Ask not what your country can do for you—ask what you can do for your country."

As President, Kennedy showed great compassion and supported the rights of all Americans. He set up the Peace Corps to help people in countries around the world. In 1962 he ordered United States Navy ships to surround Cuba to keep out Russian weapons. Russia backed down and removed the missiles they already had set up in Cuba.

President Kennedy was assassinated on November 22, 1963, in Dallas, Texas, by Lee Harvey Oswald. The whole world mourned the fallen President, a hero to millions of people.

Name _____ Date _____

If I Were President

Congratulations! You have just won the election. You're going to be President of the United States, and you are going to live in the White House! Now a newspaper reporter wants to interview you and find out what you think of your new life as President! Fill in your answers to the reporter's questions.

Reporter: Now that you are President, how do you think your life will change?

You: _____

_____

Reporter: What's the best thing about being President?

You: _____

_____

Reporter: What's the worst thing?

You: _____

_____

Reporter: This must be a wish come true for you. Are there any other wishes you have now?

You: _____

_____

Reporter: Thank you very much. And good luck in the White House!

MARTIN LUTHER KING, JR. (1929–1968)

No dream is more famous than the one Martin Luther King, Jr., described for more than 200,000 people at the Lincoln Memorial in Washington, D.C. On August 28, 1963, King held the world's attention as he said: "I have a dream that one day on the red hills of Georgia the sons of former slaves and the sons of former slave owners will be able to sit down together at the table of brotherhood.

"I have a dream that my four little children will one day live in a nation where they will not be judged by the color of their skin, but by the content of their character."

Martin Luther King, Jr., was born on January 15, 1929, in Atlanta, Georgia, into a world that tried to convince him he was inferior to white people just because he was African American. He had seen that African Americans were not treated as equals to whites under United States law. In fact, the so-called "Jim Crow" laws legally separated African Americans and whites in such public places as schools, restaurants, hotels, trains, buses, and entire areas of southern cities. African Americans were discriminated against for no other reason than the color of their skin.

But King listened harder to the voice of his Baptist minister father than to the voices of prejudice. He believed his parents when they told him he was just as good as anyone else. He spent his life working to make the rest of the world realize that all people are equal regardless of race.

Like his father and his mother's father, King became a Baptist minister. He graduated from Morehouse College and then continued his studies at Crozer Theological Seminary in Chester, Pennsylvania. It was the first time he had ever gone to school with white students. And it was at Crozer that he first read about a man from India named Gandhi. He learned about Gandhi's peaceful protests, fighting the British rulers—not with guns, but with nonviolent action such as blocking traffic by lying across the main roads. King learned that nonviolence was more effective than violence in winning rights for people. He began his own civil rights movement in 1955, leading his people in a boycott of buses in Montgomery, Alabama. The boycott worked, and soon African Americans were allowed to sit anywhere they liked on the buses.

In his short lifetime, King led hundreds of boycotts and marches to gain freedom and voting rights for African Americans. In 1964 he was chosen Man of the Year by *Time* magazine. The following year he became the youngest winner of the Nobel Peace Prize. On April 4, 1968, King went to Memphis, Tennessee, to lead a freedom march. He was assassinated by James Earl Ray. King left behind a dream of equality for all people.

Name _____ Date _____

Dreams Of A Better World

Martin Luther King, Jr., stood on the steps of the Lincoln Memorial and spoke to more than 200,000 people. He dreamed of freedom for all people. Use this space to write about your dreams for making the world a better place.

_____

_____

_____

_____

_____

_____

_____

_____

_____

_____

_____

_____

_____

_____

MAYA LIN (1959–)

When it comes to monumental achievements, Maya Lin's design for the Vietnam Veterans Memorial in Washington, D.C., is one of the most notable. Also called "The Wall," the sleek, black marble structure is engraved with 58,000 names of soldiers who died or were declared missing in action in the Vietnam War. Visiting "The Wall" is an emotional experience for all who walk past it and read the names. As remarkable as the monument is, the fact that Lin was only twenty-one years old when her design entry was selected from nearly 1,500 designs submitted to a nationwide competition.

Lin was born on October 5, 1959, in Athens, Ohio. Her parents were Chinese immigrants who came to the United States in the late 1940s. Lin combined her talents in art and mathematics in her studies of sculpture and architecture at Yale University. She was a senior at Yale in October 1980 when a group called the Vietnam Memorial Fund announced a $20,000 prize for the winner of a contest to design a memorial honoring Vietnam veterans.

Lin began by studying the history of ways architecture helps people deal with the pain of loved ones dying. She studied the journals of soldiers who fought in World War I. She visited the place where the memorial was to be built. Two acres of sloping space between the Lincoln Memorial and the Washington Monument inspired Lin to create a low wall set into the ground.

Her design of the long, black wall was approved by the committee and by the government. But one group led by a Vietnam veteran declared the wall an insult to American soldiers who had served in Vietnam. Instead of a black monument, which he said was the color of shame, sorrow, and degradation, he wanted the memorial to be white. Those who objected to Lin's design wanted a flag and another, more traditional memorial near the site. Lin told a reporter at *People* magazine that putting other elements near her design would be "like putting mustaches on other people's portraits."

Construction began in March 1982, after a compromise was reached. The color and shape would remain true to Lin's design. The flag and a second memorial would be placed near the entrance area, far from the wall. All the arguing over her design made Lin vow never to create another memorial. However, positive public response to her creation encouraged her to design another remarkable monument, the Civil Rights Memorial in Montgomery, Alabama.

Lin now spends her time on architectural and sculpture projects. She prefers to stay out of the spotlight and be left alone to work. Lin is an artist who always puts her art first.

ACTIVITIES

Design a Monument Maya Lin combined her studies of art and architecture to create the Vietnam Veterans Memorial. Give your students all the materials they need to design a monument to the greatest day, event, or person in their lives. Provide the usual markers, crayons, and paper. But add unexpected supplies such as gift boxes, juice cans, feathers, plastic containers, and fabric scraps. Let imaginations create a monumental experience for all!

Learn About Local Monuments Most towns have memorials, monuments, plaques, or markers that serve as reminders of a person, group, or event of importance to the town. Check with the local historical society or library to find such points of interest in your school's town. Take a field trip to the spot or have students visit it on their own time. Have students write a paragraph or two about something in their town which they feel should be memorialized.

Create a Class Time–Capsule Memorialize a great class and a great year! Have each student bring in something that represents him or her at this time: a recent photograph, a favorite comic strip, or just a piece of paper with his or her name written on it. On one sheet of paper, collect the signatures of each class member including the teacher's. Add other items that represent the class: field trip souvenirs, class–play programs, school newspaper articles. Put all the items in a shoebox or a large glass jar. Wrap the box or jar in plastic and bury it where it can be dug up again sometime in the future.

CHRISTA McAULIFFE (1948–1986)

Ten ... nine ... eight ... seven ... This was the countdown to a dream come true for a schoolteacher named Christa McAuliffe. It seemed unbelievable that she was strapped into her seat aboard the space shuttle *Challenger*. Next to her were five men and one other woman. McAuliffe and Gregory Jarvis were the only two civilians on board—the first ever to be included on a space flight. *... six ... five ... four ...* This was the countdown to a history-making moment which McAuliffe knew she would never forget. *... three ... two ... one ...* This was the countdown to the worst disaster in the history of the United States space program. On January 28, 1986, the *Challenger* exploded seconds after takeoff from Cape Canaveral, Florida. All seven aboard were instantly killed before the eyes of millions of people watching on television.

There had been a lot of excitement over the *Challenger's* planned flight because of those selected to be on board. The National Aeronautics and Space Administration (NASA) believed it would be easier to get the additional money needed for space missions if an ordinary citizen joined the astronauts on a flight into space. So in 1984, President Ronald Reagan announced a search for a schoolteacher to join the space mission.

In her usual "Go for it!" spirit, McAuliffe applied along with 11,000 other American teachers. In April 1985, she learned she was chosen as a finalist to be tested at the Johnson Space Center in Houston, Texas. On July 19, 1985, Vice-President George Bush named McAuliffe as the teacher chosen for the *Challenger* flight.

McAuliffe was born Sharon Christa Corrigan in Boston, Massachusetts. A good student and popular with her peers, she grew up during the formative years of the space program. Like most Americans in 1961, she watched the first astronaut, Alan Shepard, go into space. From then on, McAuliffe followed the progress of the space program and even told a friend that someday she would like to take a ride in space. By the time her opportunity arrived, she was married, the mother of two children, and a social studies teacher at Concord High School in Concord, New Hampshire.

After passing all the written and in-flight tests, McAuliffe met the *Challenger* astronauts. She was immediately accepted and treated as part of the team. She spent many hours in training, learning what to do in case of an emergency and how to eat, sleep, and live in space.

At last the flight-day came. McAuliffe said good-bye to her family and boarded the *Challenger*. Seventy-three seconds into the flight, the ship exploded. There were no survivors. McAuliffe will always be remembered for her spirit of adventure and her great determination to participate in the space program.

ACTIVITIES

On Your Mark Getting ready to travel in space is hard work. The first thing astronauts must do is make sure their bodies are in excellent shape. Take the class outside or to a large open space and lead them in an exercise program.

Get Set Packing for space travel could take awhile. Better get started now! Have students make a list of everything they would bring with them for a trip to the moon.

Go! Space may look empty from Earth. But from the window of a space shuttle, what wonders would one see? Have students draw pictures of what they might observe while traveling in space.

Risky Business Christa McAuliffe had always dreamed of traveling in space. She also knew it could be very dangerous. She was a woman with a pioneer spirit and a desire to explore new horizons. Ask students to debate whether private citizens should be allowed to take the same risks as trained astronauts.

GRANDMA MOSES (1860–1961)

By the time most people have reached a certain age, they are content to relax and just enjoy the freedom to do nothing. Anna Mary Robertson Moses, better known as Grandma Moses, started a career as a painter when she was in her seventies and continued to paint her now-famous primitive pictures for the rest of her life.

Grandma Moses was born in the mountains of Washington County, New York, a few months before Abraham Lincoln became President. She grew up on a farm in a family of ten children. When she was a child, she painted red landscapes using the red paint her father used for marking his sheep.

When she was twelve years old, she left home to work as a hired girl. She learned to cook, keep house, and make her own way in the outside world. Work was her main source of education. She admitted years later that her life was very hard. In 1887 she met and married a farmer named Thomas Salmon Moses. They lived near Staunton, Virginia, where she gave birth to ten children. Only five of them lived to be adults.

After eighteen years, the family returned to New York to live on a farm in Eagle Bridge. Thomas Moses died in 1927, but Grandma Moses continued to run the farm until her hands were too crippled by arthritis to do the farm chores. Grandma Moses was old enough to retire, but the one thing she never learned was how to sit still.

Painting became the activity that occupied her hands, mind, and time. For five or six hours a day, Grandma Moses worked on her brightly colored scenes of the countryside in upstate New York and other scenes from her memories of life in Virginia. In 1938 New York art collector Louis Caldor stopped at a drugstore in the town of Hoosick Falls, New York. He saw four of Grandma Moses's paintings in the window and inquired if there were any more. The manager pulled about a dozen additional paintings from the back room. Caldor purchased all the works immediately. He inquired about the artist and went to meet her the next day. What a surprise it was for him to discover that a seventy-eight-year-old woman had painted all the pictures. Right then and there he bought almost everything she had painted.

Caldor took Grandma Moses's work back to the New York galleries and showed them to various people. In 1940 the Galerie St. Etienne organized a one-woman show of thirty-four of her paintings. From then on, Grandma Moses became known as one of America's national treasures. Through her joyful work, she shared her feeling that it was magical just to be alive.

Grandma Moses continued to paint until her hands were too weak to hold a brush. She entered a nursing home in July 1961 after falling down at home in Eagle Bridge. On December 13, at the age of one hundred and one, Grandma Moses died, leaving her work as a reminder that it's never too late to start something new.

ACTIVITIES

Celebrate Grandma Day Grandma Moses began the most interesting phase of her life when she was in her seventies. Select a Grandma Day to honor Grandma Moses. Invite grandmothers to come to class and spend a morning with their grandchildren. Encourage the grandmas to share stories of their younger days with the class as well as new interests they developed in their later years.

Paint Like Grandma Moses Bring in samples of Grandma Moses's paintings. At first glance, her style can appear to be very primitive—some said even a child could paint as well. Give your class the chance to try it. Suggest a summer, winter, spring, or fall scene to paint. Hang the results around your room.

Interview a Grandparent That's the assignment for the class. Work together on the questions to ask and create a journalist's worksheet. Have each student interview an elderly person and fill in the worksheet to share with the class. Ask what different jobs or careers the person held and what he or she is doing now.

WOLFGANG AMADEUS MOZART
(1756–1791)

Wolfgang Amadeus Mozart is recognized by historians of music as one of the world's greatest composers of the classical period. But being great did not mean Mozart had an easy life. The fact that he composed more than 600 works did not save him from dying in poverty before his thirty-sixth birthday. The attention his work deserved did not come in his lifetime. Mozart today is perhaps best known for his operas *The Magic Flute, Don Giovanni,* and *The Marriage of Figaro,* and for his serenades, symphonies, concertos, and his *Requiem.*

The amazingly talented Mozart was born in Salzburg, Austria, on January 27, 1756. It was not surprising that he was musical since his father was the leader of a local orchestra. Both Mozart and his sister Nannerl were gifted. But when young Mozart learned to play the harpsichord at age four and began composing music at age five, his father realized that the boy was more than just musical. He was a true genius. His father Leopold was dedicated to providing both his son and daughter with the best musical education possible. They never went to school, but instead toured Europe as child prodigies.

The first tour was to Munich and Vienna in 1762. Later journeys took the boy wonder to Paris, London, and Italy. In 1764 Wolfgang's first piano and violin sonatas were printed, and three years later he received his first opera commission. The great talent he exhibited and his young age brought him to the attention of other well-known composers and the archbishop of Salzburg. In 1769, when Mozart was only thirteen, he followed in his father's footsteps and began working as a musician for the archbishop. It was Wolfgang's job to compose pieces for special occasions and to be available to entertain important guests. But his concert tours took him away from Salzburg too often, and the archbishop objected strongly. In 1781, despite Mozart's proven ability to compose operas, symphonies, masses for churches, and many other kinds of work, he was fired by the archbishop.

Mozart left Salzburg and went to Vienna where he struggled to earn a living teaching music, performing in concert, and composing concertos for his own use. He married Constanze Weber in 1782 and enjoyed a great success with his opera *The Marriage of Figaro.* Unfortunately, the public was less impressed by Mozart, the adult, than by Mozart, the child prodigy. He couldn't earn enough to save himself from a pauper's funeral when he died of a blood disease on December 25, 1791.

Name _____ Date _____

 # Music, Music, Music!

You don't have to be a musical genius like Mozart to know the score. In fact, you don't even have to know how to carry a tune. Just use your pencil and fill in the answers to this musical quiz.

1. Name three instruments that start with the letter "T."

_____

2. Name the instrument that is the homonym of the word *symbols*.

_____

3. Who stands in front and directs the orchestra?

_____

4. What instrument are you playing if you "tickle the ivories"?

_____

5. Name a wind instrument.

_____

6. Name a percussion instrument.

_____

7. Name a string instrument.

_____

8. Name one type of music.

_____

9. Name your favorite song.

_____

10. Name your favorite singer or group.

_____

Possible answers: conductor, cymbals, drum, French horn, jazz, piano, trombone, trumpet, tuba, violin.

FLORENCE NIGHTINGALE (1820–1910)

Her wealthy British parents were in the third year of their honeymoon in Europe when Florence Nightingale was born; she was named after the Italian city. The life that she and her sister Parthenope were born into was a social whirl full of parties and gatherings of the rich. From the beginning, Nightingale felt separate from the world of wealth and material things. She thought there must be more to life than what money could buy. For her, nursing became more important than anything else. Taking care of the sick and the war-wounded provided Nightingale with a profession that satisfied her search for life's meaning. It also was a profession that shocked and horrified her family.

In the middle 1800s, nursing was thought of as maid's work. A nurse's main function was to hold the hands of dirty, dying soldiers or diseased patients. But in 1837, when Nightingale was sixteen, she believed she heard God's voice calling her to His service. While her mother put all her energy into trying to introduce her daughters into the high society in which they lived, Florence Nightingale struggled with the choice of making a proper marriage or living a life devoted to the poor and sick.

In 1844 Nightingale began visiting hospitals and training as a nurse. She studied for a short time with the Sisters of St. Vincent de Paul in Alexandria, Egypt, and at the Institution for Protestant Deaconesses in Germany. But her great talent was in administration.

In 1854 she organized a hospital unit of thirty-eight nurses for the Crimean War. Carrying a lantern as she walked through rows of wounded bodies, she touched the lives of hundreds of soldiers. She introduced new standards of sanitary conditions and demanded and received the necessary supplies to provide quality nursing care. In 1860, with money given to her for her war services, she founded the Nightingale Training School for Nurses. For the rest of her life, she gave hospitals advice on nursing, sanitation, and hospital management.

"The Lady With the Lamp," the mother of modern nursing, died at the age of ninety on August 13, 1910.

ACTIVITIES

First Aid First Put together a complete first-aid kit for the classroom. Explain what each supply is used for and how to use it properly.

Red Cross Guest Invite someone from the Red Cross to come and speak about blood donations and other important health issues.

Go to the Hospital Arrange for a field trip to a hospital. A tour of the local hospital can help ease fears.

Is There a Nurse in the House? If any class parent is a nurse, invite him or her to talk about the profession and perhaps give a demonstration of what to do for a bleeding cut.

Get Well Fast Have the class make get-well cards for a classmate who is sick or for children who are in the hospital for an extended stay.

SANDRA DAY O'CONNOR (1930–)

As one of nine Supreme Court justices, Justice Sandra Day O'Connor is a member of the most powerful judicial body of the United States government. The justices have the last legal word on such major constitutional issues as civil rights. They are given lifetime tenure by the Constitution and can only be removed from their job by impeachment. Most members of the Supreme Court are not very well-known, but because of her status as the first woman on the highest court of the land, O'Connor is a celebrity.

Sandra Day was born March 26, 1930, in El Paso, Texas. She was raised on a huge cattle ranch owned and operated by her parents. Living on a ranch made her very self-sufficient. She learned to repair fences, ride horses, rope steers, and still be an excellent student. At age sixteen, she completed high school and was accepted at Stanford University.

She graduated from Stanford University in 1950 and two years later earned a law degree from the same university, where she also met and married John O'Connor. Having graduated third in her law class, she should have found it easy to get a job with a prominent law firm, but because she was a woman O'Connor was not hired.

Lacking such a position, O'Connor accepted a job as a deputy counsel in San Mateo, California. But when her husband joined the Army and was sent to Germany, she went with him and worked there for two years. When the O'Connors returned to the United States, O'Connor's husband opened a law office in Phoenix, Arizona. They had three sons, and O'Connor took time out to be a full-time mother.

In 1965 she went back to work as an assistant attorney general for Arizona. In 1969 O'Connor was appointed to a vacant seat in the Arizona Senate. She was re-elected in 1970 and 1972. She is remembered as being an excellent debater with an overwhelming amount of knowledge. In 1974 she left the Senate and ran for a superior court judgeship. As a judge she was tough but compassionate. State Republican leaders watched her carefully, and supported her Supreme Court appointment when President Reagan announced her name on July 7, 1981. In September 1981, she became the Supreme Court's first woman justice.

ACTIVITIES

You Be the Judge Set up a mock trial. Select a panel of judges to be the Supreme Court. Let one half of the class represent a lawyer for the prosecution and the other half represent a lawyer for the defense. Use real events and issues in history, such as the Boston Tea Party. Can its destruction of property be justified as free speech used to protest taxation without representation? Let this court decide what is fair.

First Women Sandra Day O'Connor is the first woman Supreme Court justice. Have the students research and report on other women who were first to do something remarkable. Examples: Sally Ride, first woman astronaut, and Elizabeth Blackwell, first woman doctor.

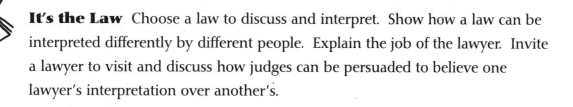

Careers for Life The job of a Supreme Court justice is guaranteed for life. Discuss what makes a good job. Ask students to debate the advantages and disadvantages of staying in the same career for a lifetime. Discuss various career opportunities that exist and what people must do to prepare for those careers.

Career Day Parents are an excellent resource for career information. Invite parents to visit the class and share information about their particular jobs.

It's the Law Choose a law to discuss and interpret. Show how a law can be interpreted differently by different people. Explain the job of the lawyer. Invite a lawyer to visit and discuss how judges can be persuaded to believe one lawyer's interpretation over another's.

ROSA PARKS (1913–   )

At the end of the first day of December in 1955, Rosa Parks, of Montgomery, Alabama, was bone tired. She had worked since early morning ironing pants and sewing cuffs in hems. Her back ached. Her neck was sore. Her feet hurt. It was a relief to get on the bus heading toward home. There was one seat left in the section at the middle where "colored" folks were allowed to sit if no white person had to stand. Parks felt lucky to get that last seat. Then the bus driver noticed some white people were standing. The driver ordered four African Americans, including Parks, to give up their seats. Parks was too tired to stand. She refused and was arrested and charged with disobeying the segregation laws of Alabama. The arrest of Parks made history and led to the passing of the Civil Rights Act by Congress in 1957. Parks became known as the "mother of the modern civil rights movement."

When Rosa Parks was born on February 4, 1913, in Tuskegee, Alabama, life was dangerous for southern African Americans. They were treated harshly and often threatened. In the South, African-American churches were burned down. African-American people were chased and lynched. And African Americans were forced to stay separated from whites in southern schools, restaurants, and all public places.

Parks never completely accepted such injustices toward herself or her people. When she was a young girl and was pushed from behind by a white boy, she pushed him back. His mother asked how she dared to push a white boy. Parks replied, "I don't want to be pushed by your son or anyone else."

When she was fifteen, Parks graduated from Booker T. Washington Junior High School and then took classes at Alabama State Teachers' College for Negroes. In 1932 she married a barber named Raymond A. Parks. Rosa Parks worked as an office clerk, a tailor's assistant, an insurance saleswoman, and a youth advisor for the National Association for the Advancement of Colored People. Her most difficult job was registering African Americans for the Montgomery Voters League. It was hard for many poor people to find the money to pay the poll tax, but Parks's efforts were successful. She was highly respected for her work in the community.

On the day that she was arrested for refusing to give up her seat on the bus, the community and the whole country were outraged. The incident touched off a thirteen-month long boycott of the bus system by African Americans and supporters of the civil rights movement. Martin Luther King, Jr., led the protest. Finally the Jim Crow laws, which prohibited African Americans from being integrated with whites, were ruled illegal by the Supreme Court. Parks is credited with contributing greatly to their final collapse.

Name _____ Date _____

Who's A Hero?

Rosa Parks made history when she refused to give up her seat on the bus. She became a hero to many African Americans because of her courage to challenge a system she did not believe was right. Not all heroes are so famous. There are heroes all around us. Who's a hero to you?

A hero to me is someone who _____

My hero is _____

This person is a hero to me because _____

The qualities I think a hero should have are _____

_____

I admire this person because _____

_____

Does a hero have to be perfect? _____

The most important ability a hero should have is _____

If I had this ability I would _____

_____

_____

_____

_____

POCAHONTAS (1595?–1617)

Captain John Smith was just about to have his head smashed with a stone club when the young Pocahontas saved his life. The Native American girl was only about twelve years old when she threw herself between her father, Chief Powhatan, and Smith, the leader of the settlers of Jamestown, Virginia. The story has been told and retold in books, movies, and paintings. Whether it is true or not doesn't seem to matter. It has become a legend in the history of peace-keeping efforts between the English and the Native Americans in Virginia.

Pocahontas, which means "playful one," used to visit the English settlers at Jamestown. She and John Smith became good friends after she saved his life. He gave her beads and other gifts. When the settlers faced a winter without food, she brought them corn.

Pocahontas, whose real name was Matoaka, married a Native American chief when she was about fourteen years old. After her marriage she was not seen in the colony for three years. During that period, Chief Powhatan grew angry with Smith and the settlers for taking more food and leaving little for his tribe. Fighting broke out, and Chief Powhatan captured and held some settlers as prisoners. In 1613 Pocahontas was captured by Captain Samuel Argall. She was taken to Jamestown where she was held as a hostage for her father's English prisoners.

Her time at Jamestown changed Pocahontas. She converted to Christianity and was baptized as Rebecca. A settler named John Rolfe fell in love with her. After getting permission both from the English governor and from her father, Rolfe married Pocahontas in April 1614. The marriage brought peace between the settlers and the Native Americans for the next eight years.

In 1616 Pocahontas went to England with her husband and several other Native Americans. She was introduced as a princess and presented to the king and queen. While waiting to return to America, Pocahontas became ill with smallpox. She died in 1617 and was buried at Gravesend, England. Pocahontas and Rolfe had one son, Thomas Rolfe, who was educated in England. In 1640 he returned to Virginia where he became quite wealthy. Many people claim to be descendants of Pocahontas, and the story of her bravery continues to be told.

Name _____ Date _____

Friends Forever

Pocahontas and Captain John Smith became good friends. She saved his life and brought him food; he gave her gifts. Do you think you are a good friend to someone? These questions may help you find out. Circle your answers.

1. There are two hungry people—you and a friend—and only one candy bar. The candy bar is yours. You: a) hide it; b) divide it in half and share; c) eat the whole thing and say you're just trying to save your friend's teeth from decay; d) other.

2. Sssssshhhh! Your friend told you a secret and you promised to keep it. Another friend says, "If you don't tell me, I won't be your friend anymore." You: a) tell the secret; b) start crying and run home; c) don't tell the secret but do tell the other friend that good friends keep secrets no matter what; d) other.

3. You want to go outside and play, but your friend wants to stay inside and play video games. You: a) compromise and do both; b) unplug the video games and say, "Oh, I guess it must be broken"; c) only play the video games but act angry the whole time; d) other.

4. Your friend just won first place in the Science Fair. You: a) feel proud of your friend and say, "Congratulations!"; b) go home before you have to say anything; c) secretly wish someone else had won; d) other.

What answers would you like your best friend to give?

_____

_____

_____

_____

MARCO POLO (1254?–1324?)

In the year 1271, Marco Polo set out with his father and his uncle on what was the longest "shopping trip" of the Middle Ages. Like many Venetians, the Polos were merchants. Niccoló Polo and his brother Maffeo could not afford to pay someone else to do their buying and selling for them. Instead, they traveled far and wide in search of new goods to sell. The three Polos left the harbor of Venice, Italy, and were gone for twenty-four years!

As a child, Marco Polo had not always known where his father and uncle were. All he knew was that they were gone for years at a time. When he was fifteen years old, his father and uncle returned to Venice. They had been all the way to China! The two brothers had met the great and wealthy ruler Kublai Khan. They had returned to Venice only to do a favor for Kublai Khan. He wanted the brothers to ask the pope to send one hundred educated churchmen to China. Because the pope had died while they were gone, the Polos had to wait two years for a new pope to be elected. The brothers brought gifts from Kublai Khan to the new pope, but he could only spare two friars.

In 1271 three Polos, Niccoló, Maffeo, and seventeen-year-old Marco set out by boat for Palestine. From there they went by caravan across Asia, all the way to Kublai Khan's court at Peking, China.

Marco Polo and Kublai Khan were both interested in learning about other people, other religions, and other ways of life. The two became friends, and Kublai Khan sent Polo to represent him on special missions. In his travels throughout China, Polo discovered many new inventions which had not found their way to Europe yet: paper money, eyeglasses, firecrackers, a printing system, and even a compass.

Polo was twenty-one years old when he arrived in China, and he stayed there for seventeen years. When Kublai Khan grew too old to be assured of his continuing power, the Polos decided it would be safer to return home. In 1292, two years before Kublai Khan died, the Polos headed home, reaching Venice in 1295. They had been gone so long that even their relatives didn't recognize them.

In 1296 a war broke out between Genoa and Venice. Marco Polo was sailing in an armed merchant ship and was captured. While he was held prisoner in Genoa, he wrote his book *Description of the World*. In the book he reported on all his travels— some said he even wrote about places he had never really seen.

Marco Polo died at the age of seventy. His adventures may have inspired Christopher Columbus to sail in search of the New World more than a hundred years later.

Name _____ Date _____

Marco Polo's Big Search

Marco Polo and his father and uncle were merchants. They left their home in Venice, Italy, and were gone twenty-four years, exploring China and searching for new goods to sell. There are ten items from China hidden in this marketplace scene. Can you help Marco Polo find them? Look for: a pair of eyeglasses, two firecracker rockets, a jar of oil, a compass, a straw hat, a teapot, a fan, an umbrella, and a bag of spices. Mark each item with an X.

DIEGO RIVERA (1886–1957)

Although he came from a wealthy and educated family, Diego Rivera grew up to be a painter of the common people, showing art away from museums and putting it on the sides of public buildings for everyone, rich or poor, to enjoy. Those who knew him when he was growing up in Mexico City, Mexico, would not be surprised that Rivera became famous for his great mural paintings. His first drawings were done on the walls of his parents' house. When his mother finally tired of filling buckets with soap and water to wash away Rivera's work, his father covered the walls of the guest room with blackboards. Once that was done, Rivera could draw and draw without having to listen to anyone's complaints.

When he was eleven years old, Rivera became the youngest student at the San Carlos Academy of Fine Arts in Mexico City, where he had received a scholarship. While it was difficult for him to pay attention to his regular studies, he had no trouble at all listening to lengthy lectures on painting techniques, composition, color, and proportion. He excelled at the academy and, when he was thirteen, was awarded a full scholarship in recognition of his talent. At San Carlos he received formal training. But it was a local printer and engraver who illustrated popular Mexican folk songs and prayers for the poor who first introduced Rivera to art "for the people."

Rivera's student career at San Carlos ended abruptly when he was expelled for leading demonstrations in favor of workers. His independent spirit enabled him to hitchhike across Mexico sketching and painting along the way. On his journey, he met peasants whose lives touched his heart. It was these common people who became the subjects of many of his paintings.

From 1907 to 1910, and then again from 1911 to 1921, he traveled through Europe, working in several countries. He was influenced by the work of El Greco and Goya and became friends with the artist Picasso. While in Europe he became convinced that a new form of art should be created for the public. When he returned to Mexico in 1921, he hired several younger artists to help him paint large murals dealing with the life, history, and problems of his country. He painted in the National Palace and in the Palace of Cortés at Cuernavaca in Mexico. His popularity spread to the United States when he painted frescoes in the Stock Exchange and in the Fine Arts Building in San Francisco as well as in the Detroit Institute of Arts.

Diego Rivera died on November 24, 1957, and his funeral was attended by thousands of men, women, and children. Both the poor and the wealthy paid their respects to the man whose art was a plea for equality and justice.

Name _____ Date _____

This Space Is Reserved For You!

Diego Rivera was an artist. He created a new kind of mural which showed the dreams and lives of common people. All artists begin with a blank canvas. This is your blank canvas. Create anything you want to here.

JACKIE ROBINSON (1919–1972)

To become a baseball star, Jackie Robinson had to practice a lot. Throwing, catching, fielding, and hitting the ball were very important skills to perfect. But even more important was practicing self-control when others called him hurtful names, intentionally knocked him down on the field, and purposely pitched well-aimed balls at his head. As the first African American to play major-league baseball in the twentieth century, Robinson had to sidestep the insults of prejudiced fans. Robinson had that special courage. That's why he has been called the bravest man in baseball.

Jack Roosevelt Robinson was born on January 31, 1919, in a shack in rural Georgia. When he was a baby, his share-cropper father ran off and left the family. His mother Mallie became the head of the household. When Robinson was sixteen months old, Mallie moved the family out of segregated Georgia to California, where schools were integrated.

From the time he was a young boy in Pasadena, California, Robinson showed genuine talent in almost all sports. His ability to concentrate made his practice rewarding. His three brothers and one sister were also athletic, but Robinson stood out. He was more determined and willing to keep practicing even after everyone else had quit.

After becoming a star in baseball, football, basketball, and track at Muir Technical High School, Robinson went to Pasadena Junior College. In 1938 he set a junior-college record in the broad jump and helped make his baseball team the junior-college champions. In 1939 he went to the University of California at Los Angeles on a sports scholarship. Then he served time in the Army. At the age of twenty-six, he became a baseball player with the Kansas City Monarchs, an all-African-American team.

Branch Rickey, a coach who had been watching Robinson for years, signed him up to play with the Montreal Royals, a farm team for the Brooklyn Dodgers. On April 15, 1947, the opening day of baseball season, Robinson made history as the first African-American player in major-league baseball. He stood at first base on Ebbets Field in Brooklyn, wearing the Brooklyn Dodgers uniform with the number 42.

From that day on, he earned everyone's respect as an athlete and as a man, and in 1947 he was named "Rookie of the Year." In 1957, when he was thirty-eight years old, Robinson retired from baseball and spent the rest of his life working for equal rights. In 1962 he became the first African American to be inducted into the National Baseball Hall of Fame. Ten years later, he was honored at Dodger Stadium in Los Angeles when the Dodgers retired his number, making 42 Robinson's number forever. On October 24 that year, Robinson died after a long struggle with diabetes and heart disease.

ACTIVITIES

Who's First? Jackie Robinson was the first African-American player in major league baseball. Who else became famous because they were the first in their field? Have students report on some famous firsts.

Who's On First? Abbott and Costello have a famous comedy routine called *Who's On First?* The subject is baseball, and the object is laughter. It is available on cassette tape. Play the tape for your class and have some baseball laughs.

Famous African Americans Prepare a bulletin board featuring other famous African Americans. Make a list of significant African Americans and have each student choose one to read about and report on to the class. Some examples to choose from are: Rosa Parks; Martin Luther King, Jr.; Maya Angelou; Toni Morrison; Arthur Ashe; and Pearl Bailey.

ELEANOR ROOSEVELT (1884–1962)

As wife of the governor of New York and then as wife of the President of the United States, Eleanor Roosevelt played a leading role in women's organizations, youth movements, consumer groups, welfare rights groups, and in the fight for better housing for minorities. She was an amazing human being whose life happened to begin in a wealthy family.

Anna Eleanor Roosevelt was born on October 11, 1884, in New York City. She was the daughter of Elliot Roosevelt and the niece of President Theodore Roosevelt. When Eleanor was eight, her father was sent away to recover from alcoholism, and her mother died. She was sent to live with her grandmother who tried to keep Eleanor separated from her father. When she was almost ten, her father died.

At the age of fifteen, Eleanor was sent to a boarding school where intelligence was more important than appearances. The confidence she gained at the school showed when Eleanor returned to America at the age of eighteen. She stood tall and slender, but it was her sharp mind that attracted her fifth cousin Franklin Delano Roosevelt, whom she married on March 17, 1905.

Over the next ten years, the Roosevelts had six children, although only five survived. Eleanor devoted all her time to being a mother and wife, as well as trying to please her very demanding mother-in-law. The day came when Eleanor wanted to do more with her life. In 1920 an amendment to the Constitution had just given women the right to vote. Eleanor cast her first vote for her husband, who was running for Vice-President on the Democratic ticket. The Democrats lost, and Eleanor turned her attention to working with the League of Women Voters.

Then a terrible crisis occurred. Franklin caught polio, a disease that made him unable to walk. Eleanor dropped everything to care for Franklin and help him grow strong enough to run for governor of New York and for President of the United States.

Overcoming her severe shyness, Eleanor Roosevelt became a popular speaker on behalf of her husband and for her own causes. In 1933 she held the first press conference ever held by a President's wife. She traveled all over the country and Europe lecturing on human rights. In 1945, while she was making a speech in Washington, Franklin Roosevelt died. Vice-President Harry Truman became President and appointed Eleanor to be a United States delegate to the United Nations. For the next fifteen years she carried the message of world peace wherever she spoke. On November 7, 1962, when she was seventy-six, Eleanor Roosevelt died.

Name _____ Date _____

First Lady's First Year

In 1933, the first year that Eleanor Roosevelt lived in the
White House, she received more than 300,000 letters.
Many of the letters asked for help. Use the space here
to write to the current First Lady to ask for her support
on issues you believe in.

_____

your street address

_____

your town, state, zip

_____

date

Current First Lady
The White House
Washington, D.C. 20500

Dear _____:

_____

_____

_____

_____

_____

_____

Sincerely,

_____

your name

BABE RUTH (1895–1948)

No matter how many years go by, Babe Ruth is never forgotten. He was baseball's first great home-run hitter as well as the game's greatest showman. His habit of pointing somewhere way out in the stands and then belting a home run right to the spot made the crowds cheer and the newspapers splash the name of Ruth across front pages. He was the hero of the 1920s, a decade known to baseball historians as "The Babe Ruth Era."

George Herman Ruth was born in Baltimore, Maryland, on February 6, 1895. The building in which he was born now houses the Babe Ruth Birthplace Museum and the Baltimore Orioles' Hall of Fame. Ruth lived on the south side of town where his father owned a saloon and his mother worked hard keeping her eight children in line. Ruth was one of the most difficult of the children to control. Eventually he was placed in a reform school called St. Mary's. It was there that Ruth became involved with baseball. Because he soon was the best player at the school, baseball became his favorite sport. In his last year at St. Mary's, Ruth hit a home run in almost every game. A Baltimore Orioles' scout named Jack Dunn came to see him play ball. Because he was

not yet twenty-one, Ruth was placed in Dunn's custody. The other players on the Orioles team called him "Dunn's newest babe." The nickname "Babe" stuck.

Even though the Orioles played well and were on their way to winning the International League pennant, the team was unable to fill the stands with fans. The only way Dunn could keep from going broke was to sell his best players. Babe Ruth was sold to the Boston Red Sox in 1914. Two years later Babe was being promoted as the best left-handed pitcher in baseball. But he was also a strong hitter. The Red Sox fans filled the stands to see Ruth play. He played every day and moved off the pitching mound to the outfield. In 1918 Ruth hit his 11th home run and established a new American League record. In fact he ended the 1919 season with 29 home runs, the only player who had hit at least one home run in every city in the league.

In 1920 Ruth was sold to the New York Yankees and hit the most home runs per season for several years. In all, he hit 714 home runs in major-league play and led the Yankees to seven pennants. Yankee Stadium was built in 1923 and came to be known as "the house that Ruth built." Ruth was traded to the Boston Braves, and in 1935 finished his playing career with them. He was the highest paid player of his era, earning $80,000 a year in 1930 and 1931. Ruth made many charitable contributions to children's hospitals before he died of cancer in 1948.

ACTIVITIES

Take Me Out to the Ball Game! Plan a field trip to a professional baseball game, a spring training game, or a local high school game.

Play Ball! Divide the class into two teams and have a world series. Invite parents to watch. Sell popcorn to earn money for class projects.

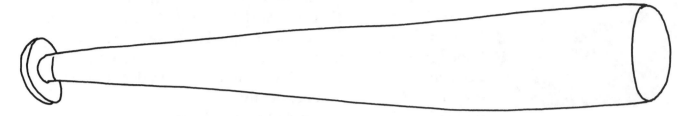

Money Talks Babe Ruth was the highest-paid player of his day, making $80,000 a year in 1930 and 1931. Nowadays sports figures earn millions of dollars. Discuss salaries for various professions. Talk about minimum wage.

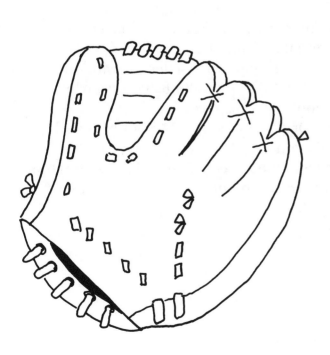

Sports Report Stage a mock sports newscast complete with interviews of "famous sports heroes." Let the students prepare their own scripts. Videotape the newscast and play it back for the class.

DR. SEUSS (1904–1991)

One of the most famous characters Dr. Seuss invented is himself—the author who is known around the world. His father had hoped he would become a doctor. He took his mother's maiden name, his own middle name, and put a "Dr." in front of it. He created the name, Dr. Seuss in 1937 with the publication of his first book, *And To Think That I Saw It On Mulberry Street.*

Theodor Seuss Geisel was born on March 2, 1904, in Springfield, Massachusetts. Geisel always had an ear for words and a drawing hand that turned doodles into cartoons. While majoring in English at Dartmouth College, he was the editor of the college humor magazine. Many of his cartoons featured his now-familiar style of creatures. After graduating from Dartmouth in 1925, Geisel went to Oxford University where he met Helen Palmer, who became his manager and then his wife. He began his career as a freelance magazine humorist and cartoonist. He moved on to jobs as an advertising illustrator and an editorial cartoonist. After receiving more than twenty-five rejection slips, his first book, *And To Think That I Saw It On Mulberry Street,* was published in 1937.

Dr. Seuss books have sold well over 80 million copies, an enormous number. *The Cat in the Hat,* published in 1957, was the first book designed as pleasurable literature for beginning readers. Dr. Seuss made it possible even for first-graders to read independently.

His style varies from verse to prose to real and made-up words. What appear to be simple nonsense stories are often moral tales dealing with greed, prejudice, and environmental concerns. Even when nonsense seems to be the theme, having fun with words is the goal.

In addition to writing and illustrating books, Dr. Seuss received many prestigious awards, including three Academy Awards, two Emmy Awards, and a Pulitzer Prize special citation. He even found a place on the adult books bestseller list with one of his last titles, *The Butter Battle Book,* which is about the arms race.

Dr. Seuss died in 1991, but his words will continue to reach generation after generation of readers who like wit, rhythm, nonsense, and perfect sense when they read.

Name _____ Date _____

On The Loose With Dr. Seuss

Dr. Seuss was famous for writing stories filled with words he made up for the sake of rhyming. Using the following made-up words, write a story or a poem of your own. It can make sense or it doesn't have to make sense at all.

GONDOOL, ZONBOOL, PRIZIX, SPRIZIX, GRAT, LAT, GRINK, PRINK, KINKYDINK, FLEEPY, REEPY, COSMOLEEPY, NEENOX, ORTOX, ZOX, QUISTER, FLISTER, GROB, CROB, ZOOLOO, MOODOO, MEEDY, FWEDDY, HIZZON, LIZZON

_____

_____

_____

_____

_____

_____

_____

_____

MOTHER TERESA (1910–1997)

Mother Teresa has chosen to help the poor while living among them. A Catholic nun, she promised to give "whole-hearted free service to the poorest of the poor." This promise has not been broken. Although her achievements often put her in the public eye, Mother Teresa shuns publicity, accepts prizes awarded her only on behalf of the poor people she serves, and takes nothing, not even credit, for the good work she does.

On August 27, 1910, a girl named Agnes Gonxha Bojaxhiu was born in Skopje, Serbia, now called Yugoslavia. One of three children, she has said that her home was so happy that she did not want to leave. As a twelve year old attending a Catholic school, she was sure she wanted to be a missionary and help the poor. Six years later her wish came true. She joined the Sisters of Loreto, a group of Irish nuns with a mission in Calcutta, India. Her first job was teaching in a high school for girls. She enjoyed her work but realized teaching was not her only calling.

Together with a group of other Catholic sisters, Mother Teresa founded the Missionaries of Charity in 1950. As a member of the group, she took a vow of poverty. Soon the sisters opened the Nirmal Hriday Home for Dying Destitutes in Calcutta where the poor could die in dignity. The Nirmal Hriday ("Pure Heart") Home was the beginning of Mother Teresa's service to the poorest of the poor. Her work included treating lepers in Calcutta's slum areas. In 1964 she "felt an involuntary calling to leave the convent and help the poor, while living among them." She and the other sisters organized a leper colony in West Bengal, funded by money received when Mother Teresa sold a limousine given to her by Pope Paul VI.

In 1979 Mother Teresa accepted the Nobel Peace Prize on behalf of the poor. She gave the prize money to the poor, as well as the money which was to be used for a celebration banquet. She observed a month of silence as a self-imposed reminder that her works were for God, not for personal recognition.

"For all kinds of diseases there are medicines and cures," she has said. "But for being unwanted, except there are willing hands to serve and there's a loving heart to love." Mother Teresa has gathered together more than 40,000 willing hands and loving hearts to serve with her in ninety-two countries around the world. Her work has generated enough donations to allow her to open other mission shelters around the world.

Name _____ Date _____

☺ Have A Good Deed Day

Mother Teresa has spent her whole life helping others. She believes that making other people's lives better also makes her own life happier. Spend one day being especially thoughtful of those around you. Keep a record of your Good Deed Day here.

Here are some examples of ways in which you might make your day a good Deed Day: sharing, caring, complimenting, helping, comforting, being thoughtful, saying "please" and "thank you," making someone laugh.

JIM THORPE (1888–1953)

James Francis Thorpe and his twin Charles Thorpe were born in a two-room cabin on a ranch near Shawnee, Oklahoma. The Thorpes felt especially blessed because on that day exactly one hundred years before, the twin's great-great-grandfather Black Hawk had been made chief of the Sac-Fox tribe. Proud of their heritage, the Thorpes also gave Jim a Sac-Fox name, which means Bright Path. He was destined to have a very bright career, ranked as one of the greatest athletes of all time.

Jim and Charlie were more than just twin brothers. They were best friends. When the boys were six years old, they were sent to the reservation boarding school. They missed home, but as long as they were together the boys were happy.

During summer vacation after their second year away, Charlie got very sick with pneumonia and died. Jim's sadness was deeper than any feeling he'd ever had except for his love for Charlie. He lost all interest in school, in friends, even in sports. After he had walked the twenty-three miles home from school twice, he was sent to the Haskell Institute in Lawrence, Kansas, where he first got involved in football and tried to get over Charlie's death. Because of his talent, he was later chosen to attend the Carlisle Indian Industrial School in Pennsylvania.

Thorpe had his first glimmer of happiness when he made the varsity squad of the football team at Carlisle. He became the best punter and drop-kicker on the team. The coach encouraged Thorpe to try other sports, and he excelled in all of them. At Carlisle, Thorpe was chosen a football All-American twice.

In 1912 Thorpe went to the Olympic games in Stockholm, Sweden. He became the first person ever to win gold medals in both the decathlon and the pentathlon as part of the United States track team, winning a total of 8,412 points out of a possible 10,000. He returned to the United States a hero. Unfortunately, and maybe unfairly, the medals were taken from him because Olympic athletes had to be amateurs. Thorpe had played with some minor-league baseball clubs for two summers, earning about two dollars a day for school. The Olympic committee stuck with their decision even though it was clear that Thorpe was not aware of the rules. With no future in the Olympics, he signed with the New York Giants baseball team and later the Cincinnati Reds and the Boston Braves. In 1920, after he returned to playing football, he helped organize what was to become the National Football League and was the NFL's first president.

In 1929, at the age of forty-one, Thorpe retired from football. In 1950 the Associated Press named him the greatest football player and greatest all-around male athlete of the first half of the century. He died of a heart attack on March 28, 1953. In 1982 the Olympic Committee returned his medals to his family.

Name _____ Date _____

And The Winner Is...You!

Jim Thorpe won two gold medals in the 1912 Olympics. He was the first person ever to win gold medals in both the decathlon and the pentathlon. Create your own "Olympic" category. Perhaps rollerblading, jumping rope, or even swinging on the swings. If you could win a gold medal for any special talent you have, what would that talent be? What would your medals look like? Design your own medals here.

SOJOURNER TRUTH (1797–1883)

In the days when slavery was a way of life for many African Americans in the United States, a slave named Isabella Baumfree was born and raised in New York State. Both her mother and father were slaves, forced to work without pay, without freedom, for a master named Hardenbergh. Her family was split up and separated as they were sold to different masters. She watched her father grow old and sick, then die without proper care. She also saw her mother become ill and die. Then she herself was sold to another family and forced to marry so that she might have children, more slaves for the master.

In 1824 Isabella heard about a new law being passed in New York declaring slavery illegal. By July 4, 1827, Isabella would be free. Her master told her that if she worked extra hard he would free her one year earlier. Isabella worked day and night to earn that early freedom. But then her hand was injured, and her master refused to keep his end of the bargain. He had lied to Isabella, and she realized all over again how terrible slavery really was.

Isabella decided to claim her own freedom. She kissed her older children goodbye and ran away with her baby to live with a Quaker family that did not believe in slavery. She missed her other children.

When her son Peter was sold to a slave owner in Alabama, Isabella became the first African-American woman in New York to sue a white man and win. Peter was freed and returned to her.

Isabella and Peter moved to New York City where there were more opportunities for work. She worked for a family there and joined the Zion African Church. Isabella felt that God had told her to preach His word. She became a traveling preacher. Before leaving New York, she changed her name to Sojourner Truth. *Sojourner* means wanderer, and she meant to wander and spread the truth, which to her was the word of God.

When Sojourner Truth spoke in her deep and powerful voice, people listened. She traveled throughout the North preaching emancipation and women's rights. She worked for proper health care for her people, and she wrote a book about her life in slavery. In 1857 she moved to a town near Battle Creek, Michigan and bought a small house for herself and her daughters.

When the Civil War came, Truth met President Abraham Lincoln, whom she admired. Lincoln signed one of her books, "For Aunty Sojourner Truth, A. Lincoln, Oct. 29, 1864." In 1865 the Civil War ended after 600,000 people had died over the issue of slavery. The Thirteenth Amendment was passed, and slavery was abolished forever. Prejudice did not end, though, and Truth spent the rest of her years working for equal rights. In 1883 she died in Michigan, where hundreds of people came to pay their respects to the former slave.

ACTIVITIES

Your Turn Each student has two minutes to express a strong opinion and try to convince the class that his or her opinion is right. After each "speech," take a vote by show of hands to see how many share the opinion, changed their opinion for or against, or have no opinion.

What Is Slavery? Anybody can be a "slave" to something. Bad habits can make someone a "slave." In what other ways could a person become a slave or feel like one? Discuss slavery and independence. Divide students into pairs and have each pair present a brief skit showing some kind of slavery.

Research Project Have students research and report on the involvement of the Quakers in the fight to end slavery.

HARRIET TUBMAN (1821?–1913)

Faith in God sometimes helped slaves endure dreary days of hard labor and living conditions unfit for humans. A favorite Bible story was about Moses, who led the Israelites from slavery. The slaves found a modern-day Moses in an escaped slave named Harriet Tubman. Like Moses leading the Israelites to freedom, Tubman led more than 300 slaves to freedom, as one of the most successful "conductors" on the Underground Railroad. This was a network of safe houses along the road to the North where runaway slaves could stop, rest, and hide.

The exact date is not known, but probably in 1821 Harriet Ross was born to Ben Ross and Harriet Green in Dorchester County, Maryland. She was the sixth of eleven children. The whole family lived together in a one-room shack. The dirt floor was covered with rags and straw for bedding. There was no furniture, no windows, no dishes, and no time to do anything except what the master ordered.

Even when Harriet was very small, she was forced to work hard. She was a messenger, a housekeeper, and a babysitter, all before she was seven years old. If she made any mistakes, she was beaten. Like many slave owners, those who owned Harriet's family wanted to keep the slaves frightened so they would continue to follow orders. But the slaves often held secret religious meetings against the orders of their masters. They studied reading and writing, which were forbidden. And the slaves tried to help other slaves who had escaped and were heading north.

Harriet often overheard the secret escape plans of slaves. She decided one day she would help make those plans become a reality. Slave owners were becoming frightened by the rebellious spirit of their slaves. Stricter laws were made forbidding slaves to gather in groups and demanding that they always carry a pass with them when they walked on public roads.

In 1844, after a long recovery from an accident which nearly killed her, Harriet married a free African American named John Tubman. Her hope that he would help her reach freedom in the North ended when they parted soon after the marriage. She kept the name Tubman and set out on her hardest job yet. She began making many, many trips back and forth between south and north, leading slaves to freedom. Her own family as well as friends and other slaves reached freedom on the Underground Railroad. Slave owners offered a $40,000 reward for the capture of the greatest "conductor" on the railroad. She was never caught and went on to fight for the Union in the Civil War. During the last years of her life, she fought for women's right to vote, helped create schools for African-American students, and helped the poor, old, and helpless. On March 10, 1913, she died a free woman in Auburn, New York.

Name _____ Date _____

Freedom Train

Harriet Tubman was the most successful conductor on the Underground Railroad, a network of safe houses for runaway slaves. Think of three reasons why freedom might be something worth struggling to attain, even if it meant facing great danger. Write one reason on each car of this Freedom Train.

MARK TWAIN (1835–1910)

In river–boating, *mark twain* means two fathoms, or a depth of twelve feet. In literature, Mark Twain means great humor and great story-telling. One familiar photograph shows Twain wearing his trademark white linen suit. During his lifetime, he also wore the clothes of a Mississippi steamboat pilot, Western miner, newspaper reporter, travel writer, editor, lecturer, and publisher. Wherever he went and whatever job he tried, he often wrote humorous stories about his experiences.

Samuel Langhorne Clemens (alias Mark Twain) was born on November 30, 1835, in Florida, Missouri. There were 2 million slaves while Twain was growing up, and he witnessed much unfair treatment of African Americans. He also grew up listening to the interesting stories the old slaves told in Hannibal, Missouri, where his family had moved in 1839.

The first time he signed a piece "Mark Twain" was in a dispatch sent to the Virginia City Territorial Enterprise on February 3, 1863. In 1864 Twain went to San Francisco and got a job as a reporter for the *Morning Call*. He also wrote for two magazines. A story called "Jim Smiley and His Jumping Frog" was published in the *New York Saturday Press* in 1865, and his name

became known in the East as well as the West. The story was later included in his first book, *The Celebrated Jumping Frog of Calaveras County and Other Sketches*. In 1866 he went to Hawaii on an assignment for the *Sacramento Union*. He sent back accounts of his experiences that had audiences roaring with laughter. When he returned to San Francisco, he began lecturing, giving live audiences a taste of his wit.

Twain is best known for his very popular books *Adventures of Huckleberry Finn* and *The Adventures of Tom Sawyer*. Both books were inspired by his early years spent earning his Mississippi River pilot license. But all of his books, articles, essays, and lectures reflect the colorful life he led traveling all over the world. He is one of only a few authors who successfully wrote for both children and adults.

In 1870 Twain married Olivia Langdon. Together they had a son and three daughters. The son died ten weeks after the second child was born. The Twains lived in an elaborate house in Hartford, Connecticut, from 1871 to 1891. The income from his books and lectures barely kept up with the expenses of his extravagant lifestyle, but being surrounded by literary friends made Twain happy.

His happiness turned to bitterness in the last twenty years of his life. While Twain was on a lecture tour in 1896, his daughter Susy died. His wife died eight years later, and his youngest daughter Jean died in 1909. On April 21, 1910, Twain died, leaving a body of work that has steadily increased in popularity. His great sense of humor never goes out of style.

ACTIVITIES

What's So Funny?   Mark Twain is one of America's greatest humorists. He made people laugh with stories taken from his own experiences and travels. Have students tell the class about the funniest things they ever saw.

Write for Laughs   Mark Twain's name became known in the East when his story called "Jim Smiley and His Jumping Frog" was published. Even the title is funny. Have students write three titles that sound funny to them. Then let them choose one title and write a short, funny story for it.

Humor Study   There are many kinds of humor—slapstick, satire, parody, one-line jokes, television situation comedies. Discuss several kinds of humor. Have students give examples for each category.

Jokes Are Us   Make a class joke book. Have each student contribute several favorite jokes. Type them up. Have students do pencil illustrations to go with some of the jokes. Put them into book form and make a copy for each student.

YOSHIKO UCHIDA (1921–1992)

Most authors write with the hope that readers will gain something from reading their work. As a Japanese-American author and illustrator, Yoshiko Uchida hopes that her work is a step toward the "creating of one world."

Uchida believes she can bring greater understanding of and respect for Japanese people through her more than thirty books for children. By writing from her own cultural heritage, she hopes "these books will help dispel long-existing stereotypic images and also increase among Japanese-American young people an understanding of their own history and pride in their identity." Her books for children all relate to her ethnic background, and most feature Japanese Americans.

Some of her books, such as her first, *The Dancing Kettle and Other Japanese Folk Tales*, are interpretations of Japanese folk tales set in old Japan. But *New Friends for Susan, Mik and the Prowler, Journey Home, Journey to Topaz*, and other books are set in modern times and deal with problems faced by today's Japanese, both in Japan and in this country. Uchida, who travels to Japan occasion- ally, has been successful in writing realistically but without bitterness about the relocation of Japanese living in the United States to restricted camps in Utah during World War II. She is equally successful at depicting other issues such as taking responsibility, respecting elders, meeting challenges, and adjusting to new situations.

Uchida was born in Alameda, California, on November 24, 1921. After graduating from the University of California, Berkeley in 1942, she was a graduate fellow at Smith College. Uchida taught at the Japanese relocation center in Utah during the Second World War and, later, at Frankford Friends School in Philadelphia.

In addition to writing books for children, she also writes for adults. For either audience, her books always include strong plots, interesting settings, well-rounded characters, intelligent dialogue, and colorful descriptions.

ACTIVITIES

Find Japan on the Map Using a world map, point out Japan.
See if students can figure out how many miles they would have
to travel from their town to Japan.

Read a Japanese Folk Tale Select one or two folk tales
from Yoshiko Uchida's book *The Dancing Kettle and Other Japanese
Folk Tales*. Compare an American folk tale to a Japanese folk tale.
Discuss the similarities.

Let's Eat Japanese Plan a field trip for lunch at a Japanese
restaurant. Or teach students how to eat with chopsticks and
try out the new skill on bowls of rice in the classroom.

Study Japanese Art Show students examples of Japanese
paintings and origami. Have them try to imitate the
delicate styles they see.

LAURA INGALLS WILDER (1867–1957)

Like many girls raised in the late 1800s, Laura Ingalls Wilder liked to sit on the floor and play with a favorite doll. She liked to run in the fields around her family's log cabin. She worried that her straight brown hair wasn't as pretty as her sister Mary's golden curls. And she liked watching her mother and father doing chores. Wilder was not so different from other pioneer girls. What was different, though, was that she grew up and became a world-famous children's book author, writing about her childhood in the "Little House" books.

Wilder's life began in a little house in the big woods on February 7, 1867, somewhere near the town of Pepin, Wisconsin. Later, Wilder wrote about the evenings in the little house in the big woods where her family sat around a fire and listened to Pa play his fiddle and tell stories. Wilder understood her father's spirit of adventure: he moved the family nine times between the years of 1874 and 1877! But to Wilder, home was not a place. Home was Ma, Pa, and her sisters Mary, Carrie, and Grace.

Wilder's family faced hardships throughout Laura's childhood. Grasshoppers destroyed their crops; snowstorms deprived them of food; the only boy born to the Ingallses died at nine months; and Pa was in and out of work. One of the worst disasters occurred when Wilder's sister Mary got scarlet fever and had a stroke, which caused blindness. Wilder became her sister's "eyes." She painted pictures with words so that her sister could "see" everything that Laura saw. They were a family of survivors.

The Ingallses were the first family to settle in the land that would become South Dakota. In 1880 and 1881, winter lasted seven months. Food ran out, and the Ingallses were starving. A young man saved them as well as other families in the area by supplying them with wheat. That was the beginning of a long courtship between Laura Ingalls and the older Almanzo Wilder.

At the age of fifteen, Wilder left home to be a school teacher. Three years later in 1885, Laura and Almanzo were married. Their daughter Rose was born one year later, and a newborn son died three years after that. Sadness seemed to surround them when two weeks later their house burned down.

In 1894 the Wilders traveled by covered wagon to Mansfield, Missouri. On the forty-five day journey, Wilder kept a diary. In 1911 her first article was published in a farm journal. In 1932, with the help of her daughter, who became a newspaper writer, Wilder's book *Little House in the Big Woods* was published. Seven books followed.

Almanzo Wilder died in 1949 at the age of ninety-two. At the age of ninety, Wilder died three days after her birthday in 1957. She left behind *The Little House on the Prairie* series which young readers have treasured ever since.

Name _____ Date _____

A Writer's Notebook

Laura Ingalls Wilder wrote about life in a house in the big woods and a little house on the prairie. She described everything about her home, her family, her school, and her surroundings. Use this page to make notes for a book you might write about your life.

Describe the place where you live: _____

_____

What color are the walls in the room where you sleep?

_____

Name three favorite things in the room where you sleep:

_____

Name the members of your family (pets included):

_____

Point out one important physical feature of each family member:

_____

How do you feel when you come home after school?

_____

What is it about your home that makes you feel that way?

_____

What would be the title of your book about growing up in your house?

_____

In one word, describe how you would feel if you found out you were moving:

_____

THE WRIGHT BROTHERS;
ORVILLE (1871–1948)
WILBUR (1867–1912)

Two *Wrights* can't make a wrong. Orville and Wilbur Wright proved that on December 17, 1903, at Kitty Hawk, North Carolina. On that great day in aviation history, the Wright brothers made the first controlled and sustained flights in a power–driven airplane. Of the four flights made that day, the first one, which was made by Orville, lasted 12 seconds. The fourth one, made by Wilbur, covered 852 feet in 59 seconds. Those times and distances may not seem like much, but if it were not for those first experiments by the two brothers, there might not be any flights today!

Orville and Wilbur, who was four years older, often argued about how things worked. When they were children growing up in Dayton, Ohio, anything mechanical held their interest. In 1878 their clergyman father gave the two boys a small toy made of cork, bamboo, and paper. It had two propellers and a rubber band to wind it up. The boys played with the skittering toy until it wore out. Then they made their own versions of it.

Neither Orville nor Wilbur graduated from high school, but both were strong readers. Their great love of mechanics occupied the brothers' minds so much that neither had time to marry. Instead they became business partners and opened first a print shop, then a bicycle shop.

Through their work with bicycles, they learned what could be used in making airplanes. When they began inventing a flying machine, there was already a lot known about engines and wings. Control was the biggest remaining problem, so they focused on that. One of their continuing arguments came from hours of studying birds in flight. Balance was the goal for the brothers, and the birds seemed to have that figured out perfectly. They applied their bird–watching knowledge to a glider they made in 1899 and continued improving their designs in kites and other gliders. Finally, their plane, the Wright Flyer, performed for an audience of four men and a boy on December 17, 1903. It was the Wright Flyer's first and last flight. After the plane had safely landed, a gust of wind blew it down the sandy runway, wrecking it. But the flight and the invention of the airplane were documented.

The Wrights refined their original design in 1904 and 1905 and built two other planes. Record–breaking flights by both brothers gained them international fame. A patent was issued in 1906, and the brothers prospered from their work.

Wilbur Wright died on May 30, 1912, of typhoid fever. Orville sold the company three years later and lived until 1948.

Name _____ Date _____

The Right Idea

The Wright Brothers were full of *Wright* ideas. They invented a flying machine. Here's your chance to write down your bright, right idea.

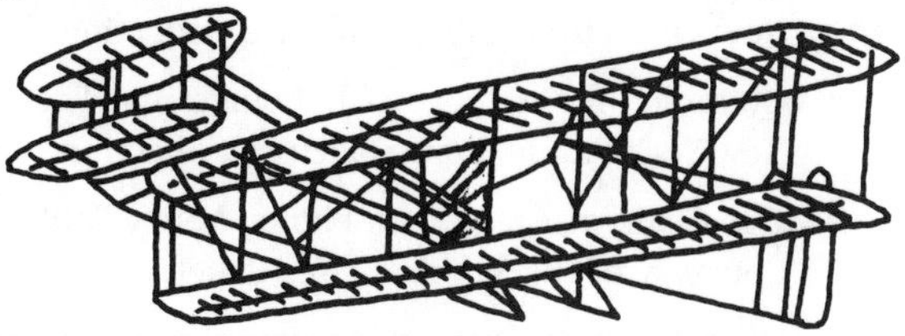

My invention is called: _____

_____

It is used for: _____

_____

It looks like this:

Photography and Picture Credits

Susan B. Anthony (page 6): Courtesy of The New York Public Library Picture Collection.

Arthur Ashe (page 8): © Jeanne Moutoussamy-Ashe, Fifi Oscard Agency, Inc.

Alexander Graham Bell (page 10): Courtesy of The New York Public Library Picture Collection.

Gwendolyn Brooks (page 12): Courtesy of The New York Public Library Picture Collection.

Evelyn Cisneros (page 14): Photo: Marty Sohl. Courtesy of the San Francisco Ballet.

Bill Clinton (page 16): Courtesy of the White House.

Marie Curie (page 18): Courtesy of The New York Public Library Picture Collection.

Albert Einstein (page 20): Photo: New York Daily News. Courtesy of the Archives, Institute of Advanced Studies.

Queen Elizabeth II (page 22): Drawing by Shi Chen. © Troll Associates, Inc.

Chris Evert (page 24): Drawing by Shi Chen. © Troll Associates, Inc.

Anne Frank (page 26): Courtesy of The New York Public Library Picture Collection.

Benjamin Franklin (page 28): Courtesy of The New York Public Library Picture Collection.

Galileo Galilei (page 30): Courtesy of The New York Public Library Picture Collection.

Mohandas Gandhi (page 32): Drawing by Shi Chen. © Troll Associates, Inc.

Jane Goodall (page 34): Drawing by Shi Chen. © Troll Associates, Inc.

Virginia Hamilton (page 36): Photo: Skylight Studios. Courtesy of The Putnam Publishing Group.

Jim Henson (page 38): © Jim Henson Productions, Inc.

Harry Houdini (page 40): Courtesy of The New York Public Library Picture Collection.

Thomas Jefferson (page 42): Courtesy of The New York Public Library Picture Collection.

Chief Joseph (page 44): Courtesy of The New York Public Library Picture Collection.

Helen Keller (page 46): Courtesy of Helen Keller International.

John Fitzgerald Kennedy (page 48): John Fitzgerald Kennedy Library.

Martin Luther King, Jr. (page 50): Drawing by Shi Chen. © Troll Associates, Inc.

Maya Lin (page 52): The Bettman Archive, Inc.

Christa McAuliffe (page 54): Photo: Keith Myers, The New York Times. Courtesy of NASA.

Grandma Moses (page 56): Portrait of Grandma Moses at the age of 89. Photo by Otto Kallir. Copyright © 1981, Grandma Moses Properties Co. New York.

Wolfgang Amadeus Mozart (page 58): Courtesy of The New York Public Library Picture Collection.

Florence Nightingale (page 60): Courtesy of The New York Public Library Picture Collection.

Sandra Day O'Connor (page 62): © The National Geographic Society, courtesy, The Supreme Court Historical Society.

Rosa Parks (page 64): Courtesy of The New York Public Library Picture Collection.

Pocahontas (page 66): Courtesy of The New York Public Library Picture Collection.

Marco Polo (page 68): Courtesy of The New York Public Library Picture Collection.

Diego Rivera (page 70): Courtesy of The New York Public Library Picture Collection.

Jackie Robinson (page 72): National Baseball Library & Archive, Cooperstown, New York.

Eleanor Roosevelt (page 74): Franklin D. Roosevelt Library.

Babe Ruth (page 76): National Baseball Library & Archive, Cooperstown, New York.

Dr. Seuss (page 78): Courtesy of Random House.

Mother Teresa (page 80): Drawing by Shi Chen. © Troll Associates, Inc.

Jim Thorpe (page 82): Courtesy of The New York Public Library Picture Collection.

Sojourner Truth (page 84): Drawing by Shi Chen. © Troll Associates, Inc.

Harriet Tubman (page 86): Courtesy of The New York Public Library Picture Collection.

Mark Twain (page 88): Courtesy of The New York Public Library Picture Collection.

Yoshiko Uchida (page 90): Photo: Deborah Storms. Courtesy of the Macmillan Children's Book Group.

Laura Ingalls Wilder (page 92): Courtesy of HarperCollins.

The Wright Brothers (page 94): Courtesy of The New York Public Library Picture Collection.